one lost boy:

HIS ESCAPE FROM
POLYGAMY

one lost boy:
HIS ESCAPE FROM POLYGAMY

DAVID BEAGLEY

CFI
Springville, Utah

ISBN 13: 978-1-59955-204-0

Published by CFI, an imprint of Cedar Fort, Inc., 2373 W. 700 S., Springville, UT 84663
Distributed by Cedar Fort, Inc., www.cedarfort.com

Cover design by Nicole Williams
Cover design © 2008 by Lyle Mortimer
Edited and typeset by Annaliese B. Cox

Printed in the United States of America

10 9 8 7 6 5 4 3 2 1

Printed on acid-free paper

Contents

Introduction

My purpose in writing this book is not to attack my parents or my brothers and sisters, but to declare to all that we must be patient with the Lord by allowing him to be in charge. We can seldom see much of our future, but Heavenly Father can. Our efforts, therefore, should be spent in aligning ourselves with his will so we can develop the necessary faith to wait on the Lord for his promised blessings. We cannot receive those blessings on demand. They are apportioned by heavenly design and in the Lord's timing. But he is never late. As we develop patience in the Lord, we begin to focus less on immediate trials and future blessings, and more on loving and serving our fellow men without consideration of reward. We must not quit traversing the path of life because we think the terrain is too rugged or the climb is too steep. Just around the next bend all the scenery could change and we could be swept up into God's loving arms. But that reunion is always preceded by our willingness to abide the heat of his refining fire. In the meantime, we must stand between the campaigns of God and Satan for our souls, and we must not cast the deciding negative vote. Safety only comes by extending that decision to God. Therein lies the essence of the eternal sifting process, the blessing and curse of agency. Ultimately, if we can endure the journey and make the proper sacrifices, we will find ourselves compensated beyond our finite imaginations.

A patriarchal blessing gives inspired counsel and insight about a person's life. My patriarchal blessing makes a clear statement that I would be known as "a man who loves the Lord," and "the time will be all too short for you to do the things that you would like to do for your fellow man."

To that end, I write this book to declare my love for the Lord and my love for my fellow man. In so doing, I know I risk the possibility of angering members of my parents' family, but I pray that they will accept truth when they hear it. Both of my parents are long deceased, and my siblings are split apart by religious intolerance, hatred, and mistrust. I wish not to offend, but to bring all who will listen into the loving arms of Christ.

CHAPTER ONE

How Much Sacrifice Is Enough?

In 1950 when I was six years old, Dad was excommunicated from The Church of Jesus Christ of Latter-day Saints for practicing polygamy. The anger my family felt toward the bishop and stake president was something I could not resolve immediately. The anger I felt toward my father for choosing polygamy as a lifestyle would not be resolved for many years more. When Bishop Hanks took each of us children aside and explained the reason for our father's excommunication, I could not have known then that my feelings of devastation and humiliation were destined to become blessings.

The roads leading to God and his blessings are as numerous as there are people. Each passage is unique. Each has as its common denominator a surrender to God's will and consummate trust that he has a plan for us. I wanted my path to lead me to happiness—a big goal for a twenty-year-old who had experienced little of it.

One night in January of 1964, as I stared out the frosty window of a California-bound passenger train, I recalled some of those earlier turns as I faced yet another detour: reassignment to a new mission. Some fourteen months earlier, when I had accepted my call for a two-year proselyting mission to northern Scotland, I was promised that if I served with all my heart, might, mind, and strength, blessings would follow. What had followed were health problems so debilitating that I was now being transferred stateside so that doctors could monitor my progress. I felt defeated. I saw no exalted purpose, none of the hoped-for blessings in my present situation. Rather, my mind was filled with confusion.

Hadn't I courageously broken polygamy's grip, given up family and friends for this mission? Hadn't I sacrificed everything to forge a new life in the true Church? Hadn't I tried to be good? What price was enough?

I made many promises to the Lord as I pleaded with him to be healed and remain in Scotland. Now I felt forgotten; I didn't even have a supportive family to empathize with my plight. Sitting alone on the train, I envisioned my fellow missionaries, some of whom had served with only a partial commitment. I, on the other hand, had paid a dear price to be a member of the Church. The gospel was lifeblood to me.

The fact that I was able to serve as a missionary was nothing short of a miracle. The last missionary from my family had been excommunicated for preaching polygamy while on his mission in Texas. Many years of bad blood between the leaders of the Church and the Beagley family had taken a natural course. Consequently, I had to endure two grueling interviews with Elder Mark E. Peterson, a member of the Quorum of the Twelve Apostles (leaders of the entire Church), who was assigned to wayward families. It was his job to determine the depth of my sincerity in abandoning my polygamist upbringing. Once he cleared my name, I bounded into my mission in full stride. No sacrifice was too great. Instead of spending preparation days tripping off to visit some castle with the entire district of elders, I remained behind to memorize discussions and scriptures. I never cheated the Lord out of a full day's work. I always tried to put in extra time. In fact, so that I would not be tempted to become distracted and worldly, I hadn't even brought a camera to Scotland, one of the most beautiful places on earth. I was determined to do everything right, and I was certain that having so served with all my heart, might, mind, and strength, my heart's desire of normalcy and happiness would follow.

Now, with my mission to Scotland abruptly ended and having been reassigned, I spent most of my two-day train ride to California asking more questions and receiving few answers. Did I have the courage to recommit to a second mission? Could I trust the Lord to extend the blessings that had so long eluded me? Where was he taking me?

Perhaps, I concluded, the answers lay in the past. Could I reach back far enough into the memory of my youth to find comfort for what appeared to be an undeserved consequence for faithfulness? By allowing myself to drift into the past, would I risk weakening my testimony of the truthfulness of the gospel of Jesus Christ? What toll would be exacted for two days of self-pity? My body was trapped on a train going west, while my heart kept pleading to return east to Scotland. Were the promised blessings a future reality or were they mere wishes? I had no choice but to return to my roots for answers.

I am the product of Mormon pioneer stock. My mother's parents had settled in Cardston, Alberta, Canada, where winters are harsh. When my mother was just eight years old, her maternal grandmother died, and so my mother assumed adult responsibilities. Later, her father moved the family to Lehi, Utah, to raise his children under the umbrella of the Church. In time, Mom graduated from high school and entered Brigham Young University, where she studied to become a teacher.

My mother, Althea Ovella Ferrell Beagley, was one of the finest women I ever knew. No woman ever walked this earth who worked harder for her children. She stood about five-foot-seven and supported a large frame. She was firm and consistent in discipline. When she spoke, each of her twelve children listened and obeyed. She had a keen sense of humor that kept us endeared to her conversation. Her smile warmed everyone around her.

At one Friday night dance, Mom met Jesse Nielson Beagley. Dad stood about six feet tall and weighed over two hundred pounds. He was a very attractive man with pleasant features that drew people to him. His hair was full, and he enjoyed combing it while admiring himself in the mirror. His speech was common and often included profanity to empha-size a point. He came from a rough background, having grown up near the copper mines of Magna, Utah. Although a member of the Church, he was mostly uncommitted, as was his family.

Dad's mother was a tobacco-chewing, cussing, coffee drinker who had often entertained Porter Rockwell (feared Mormon lawman) in her home. Visits to Grandma Beagley's home in Magna produced remark-able stories and provided me with many new swear words to add to my young vocabulary. On one visit, Grandma spoke of her pride in turning in her own husband for horse stealing. She boasted of making sure that Grandpa Beagley spent five years in the state penitentiary for being dis-honest. She seemed to do much better with his being gone so she could rule the roost.

After a period of courting, Mom and Dad were married at the county courthouse on a Saturday afternoon. Years later, due to Mom's nagging persistence, the couple was sealed in the Salt Lake Temple. Twelve chil-dren resulted from the union—nine boys and three girls. My parents made their first home in Orem, Utah. Future Utah home sites would include Tooele, the Avenues in Salt Lake City, and Wellington. We also stayed in Missoula, Montana, for three years.

Our Orem home was too small for a large family, so Dad began to construct a larger house across the street. With several of my older brothers to help, the home was soon completed. Mom was proud of her new "dream come true" and loved the neighborhood. She insisted that her young family be raised in The Church of Jesus Christ of Latter-day Saints, and Dad reluctantly went along with her desires.

In those early years it appeared as though we were a somewhat normal, happy family, active in the LDS Church. But appearances can be deceiving. My older siblings participated in family home evening and attended Gold and Green Balls—all the little things that good members of the LDS Church do. Hymns were sung in the home. When I came along—the tenth child and the seventh boy—my mother still gathered us together at her knee each morning to be instructed for at least thirty minutes in the scriptures. Dad, on the other hand, became more and more disinterested. He wouldn't accept Church responsibilities, and he eventually stopped attending the meetings altogether, claiming that someone in the ward (the local LDS congregation) had offended him. "A person can find God better in the mountains than on a church pew," he was wont to argue. By and by some of the older children began to agree with his reasoning and Sundays became barbecue or outing days, a time for baseball and picnics. Mother refused to compromise and continued to attend Church with the younger children. Although she appeared brave, inwardly she was devastated. She was losing her family, and she didn't know how to hold onto them.

Over time, our family split in half over the issue of Church activity. Many of my older brothers and sisters, now adults, were rapidly moving away from the Church due to Dad's example and his constant barrage of critical barbs. The rift between Mother and Dad also challenged parental alliances, as each child was forced to choose between them. The family was slowly being torn apart by our parents' religious preferences, and their marriage was in serious peril. But as formidable as was this challenge, nothing could have prepared my mother or us children for the trial that was to come.

One evening, while Dad was working at Geneva Steel in Orem, Utah, he spoke with a coworker who favored living with more than one woman.

The idea of polygamy struck a titillating chord in Dad. He was intrigued. The idea of plural marriage satisfied a great dilemma within him: he now saw a way to justify his censure of the Church that had so long irritated him, and he had discovered a legitimate way to commit adultery.

The Church of Jesus Christ of Latter-day Saints began practicing polygamy several years after its founding. Although many present-day Church members are descendants of polygamist families, living the principle now is unthinkable. Even in the early days of the Church, polygamy caused an uproar at the highest levels and tested even the most faithful. Nothing short of a prophetic calling to a couple and their subsequent assurance from the Lord could have prompted candidates to live such a difficult law. Consequently, only about 6 percent of the Church members ever engaged in polygamy. However, after the United States Congress passed the Edmunds-Tucker Act outlawing plural marriage, President Wilford Woodruff, in 1890, received a revelation that the practice was to end. The Manifesto was accepted by the Church in the October 1890 general conference of the Church. Most members accepted this revelation, but some held that President Woodruff was a fallen prophet, and they "went underground" to continue practicing what they considered the higher law.

So it was with Dad. Promptly after announcing that he had been "chosen by God to a better work," he began looking for other wives. My mother was devastated. Dad countered her objections with answers that he received from fundamentalist meetings in Salt Lake City. With the passage of time, something extraordinary happened—a bizarre transformation in my mother's attitude. And now, with a forty-eight hour train ride ahead of me to California, I had plenty of time to try and analyze my mother's acquiescence from active Latter-day Saint to polygamist wife.

My mother was reared to believe that you make one—and only one—lifetime choice in marriage and that you stick with that decision no matter what. This attitude may have encouraged her metamorphosis. Supporting her decision to convert to polygamy was her abhorrence for divorce. During the 1940s and 1950s, divorces were exceptional. It was rare indeed to encounter someone from a single-parent home. Although Mom threatened divorce, neither she nor my father would initiate the papers. I suppose Mom chose to sacrifice her life—her freedom, her dignity, her belief system—to salvage her marriage and try to hold her family together. Essentially she was trying to make the best of a bad situation.

5

Perhaps bearing twelve of Dad's children played a major role in her decision to stay with a sinking ship. As I stared out one of the train windows into the darkness of a wintery night, I remembered my mother's pain and wondered why I had been chosen before this life to be one of those twelve children.

Dad's first attempt at polygamy was moving two teenage sisters, whose parents had abandoned them, into our Orem home. He aggressively courted them in front of my mother. But his attempts failed due to our bishop's intervention. The girls were eventually removed. Next, Dad insisted that Mom turn our home into a day-care center to support him as he pursued his "higher calling." Providing for his present children wasn't a top priority for Dad. Because he was naturally highly persuasive, he wore my mother down, and she eventually relented.

Each month as Dad dropped by to pick up some money, I wondered, *Can't she see that she's being used?* But loneliness and her need for companionship took their toll and, like a brainwashed prisoner of war, she conceded to one thing after another until she, too, began attending fundamentalist meetings and listening to the polygamist ideology. There, the group's "priesthood leaders" soothed Mom with promises that she would always be Dad's first wife and would thus maintain a favored status. Part of that promised status was to include her in finding and accepting future wives for Dad. This turned out to be hollow and misleading. She finally caved in. She accepted callings in the group and reluctantly agreed to be one of Dad's polygamist wives.

With his wife's permission secured, Dad embraced his new life with enthusiasm. Over time, he married four more wives in secret to avoid detection by the law, for it is beneath the cloak of secrecy that the fundamentalists survive. Mom's hope that her acquiescence would improve her marriage and bind up her family was to be dashed. She and the rest of us in Dad's "first family" had merely become stepping stones to his many beds and his fathering almost fifty children. In fact, Dad became so preoccupied with increasing his "holdings" and creating progeny that he had less and less time to visit us. When he did drop in, he often didn't recognize me and mistook me for one of my brothers. My feelings for him were confused. On one hand, I was angry; I felt betrayed and abandoned. On the other hand, I wanted to love him and feel a sense of loyalty. These feelings would intensify when Dad lost his membership in The Church of Jesus Christ of Latter-day Saints.

In time, Mom stopped attending our local Church meetings altogether and began hauling us children off to support the fundamentalist group. I hated their meetings! They were filled with doomsday prophecies and focused on LDS Church bashing. Even as a young boy, I could sense the stark contrast between the fundamentalist meetings and times when I had felt the Spirit while I attended Primary in the LDS Church. I had also felt the love of Christ as I listened to my mother read from the scriptures. But, like it or not, I had been set on a course by my parents—by my father for reasons of selfishness and by my mother because of mental fatigue.

As the events of my father's apostasy unfolded, our stake president (an LDS leader with responsibilities over several congregations), Philo T. Edwards, the father of famed BYU football coach LaVell Edwards, worked with Dad for a very long time, lovingly encouraging him to hold our family together and abandon his polygamist ideas.

By this time, regardless of the efforts of many in the ward or stake, my father had tasted of the fruit of adultery and liked it. Soon, President Edwards had no alternative except to call a high council court and excommunicate my father from the Church. As an act of love and concern, President Edwards sat our family down to carefully explain the reason for the excommunication, and then he followed up by assigning Bishop Hanks to personally visit our home and check on Mother.

I was so young and confused that I was angry at both my father and the stake president. Dad had selfishly hurt my mother and me and had shattered our family. Any hope for a normal, cohesive life had been extinguished by his self-indulgent actions. But he was still my dad, and I was no different than any other young boy; I desperately needed the nurturing of a loving father. That much I knew, even at the tender age of six. Most of my older brothers and sisters viewed the stake president as having hurt my dad. The embarrassment we felt was extenuated by the fact that, in those days, excommunications were announced from the pulpit. Thereafter, the neighborhood buzzed with the news. I listened to Dad grouse about how cruel President Edwards had been for publicly humiliating him in front of his friends. I found myself confused, not knowing who to hate more.

The passenger train rolled through Nevada westward toward California in the darkness of night. Alone with my thoughts, I found sleep impossible. I recalled my entrance into the mission field. I thought I had life pretty well figured out. I had concluded that because God had tested me early in life and guided me through the twists and turns of childhood, he was leading me to the reward: a mission in Scotland. But that reward was not to last. Sickness was defeating me. My mind burned with unresolved ironies. I had endured the jolt of my father embracing polygamy. I had survived being ripped from my active LDS life, forced to live a secret life on the fringes of society—a new social structure, a new church, and new rules. I had coped with watching my family torn apart.

Now illness and reassignment?

My destination—the Lord's promised happiness—was as vividly desired in my mind as ever, but it now seemed remote. For the moment, all I could do was mine the deep caverns of my soul to try and unearth trust, because as hard as I tried, I struggled to see God standing beside me or leading me carefully along.

Does this testing go on for a lifetime? I wondered. Couldn't my Heavenly Father accept the sacrifices of my youth and ease up for a season? How much sacrifice is required? How much sacrifice is enough?

CHAPTER TWO

Short Creek

When I was eight, Mother chose to remove the family from the social pressures of our Orem neighborhood. When the family had been active in the Church, our neighbors had showed great interest in our welfare. Now that Mom had stopped attending, the community was buzzing with the speculation that Dad had finally convinced her to look the other way as he sought multiple beds. We purchased a home in the Avenues of Salt Lake City, hoping to escape the scrutiny of our Orem neighbors and also desiring to move closer to Dad. Our new house was a tall, old structure, typical of the early 1900s, with many bedrooms and lots of space. We moved in when I had just started the second grade. Two of my older brothers were in the armed forces in Korea, and four other brothers and sisters were married. Mom was left with the six younger children to raise on her own.

I loved my mother more than anything. To me, she was the epitome of strength and wisdom. She arose every morning at 4:30 to prepare the nursery for the children who would be arriving, and to make breakfast for her own children. Before retiring at 11:00 each night, she would elevate her tired feet on a broken-down footstool and let down her waist-long hair. I loved to watch her brush her hair before we both went to bed.

Mom's attempts to keep herself and her children closer to Dad failed. He rarely visited our Salt Lake City home. Mom's inability to produce any additional children and his passion for his new familial pursuits kept Dad away until the first day of each month when he came to pick up his check.

These were tough financial times for my mother. Making payments on her Orem home and a second payment in Salt Lake City had exhausted all her funds. Now she was faced with the humiliating decision of returning to Orem and all the ridicule that she had left two years earlier. She felt that she had no choice.

She had begun operating a day-care center and working long, hard hours years before when the family had lived in Orem. In a direct way, we children felt the effects of her difficult schedule. Summers were a case in point. Claiming that she needed to remove her children from the evil influences of Utah neighborhoods, Mother transported a trailer to the desert of Short Creek, Arizona, which later became known as Colorado City—a polygamist colony. Short Creek was an austere place with no running water or paved streets. At the beginning of summer, Mom would deposit us six younger children in this undeveloped desert, into the care of others, and then return to Orem to operate her business. For those long, hot months, the trailer was our home.

The community of Short Creek was located on the border of Utah and Arizona, chosen strategically so that the residents could slip from one state to another when authorities approached. In this polygamy haven, plural marriage was alive and thriving. Short Creek had many large and mostly unfinished homes where multiple families lived. The fathers were hardworking, capable breadwinners, and from a very early age, each son was expected to assist his father in his work. Daughters stayed by their mothers' sides and learned homemaking skills.

One of the admirable qualities of the Short Creek society was that the members helped each other. Like the Amish, the entire community was wont to gather at the crack of dawn on a Saturday and raise an entire barn in one day. Hundreds of men, women, and children were assigned specific tasks such as building walls, floors, roofs, carrying lumber, and cleaning up scraps.

In Short Creek, men being married to multiple wives was normal, and often these wives were sisters by birth. For the most part, the families seemed to function well and the society was effective. The children were taught to speak only when spoken to, and then only with permission from a parent. The husband was the head of the home and was to be referred to as Father, not Dad. The outside world often stood amazed that so many women could live in the same house while bearing the same man's children and get along with each other. Such unity was achieved by young ladies, who, from their birth, were raised to believe that being married to a man with multiple wives was the highest form of Godliness. The decision of whom and when to marry was strictly determined by the community leaders, and all marriages were conducted in secret. Often the new wife would not be informed of her wedding until the day before the ceremony, which was performed in a leader's home.

There was a price for this communal efficiency. In order to maintain cohesiveness and to discourage dissidence, the leadership of Short Creek kept a constant vigil to assure that outside influences did not contaminate the citizens. They were extremely controlling. The communal level of discomfort heightened when new families from the "big cities" moved into their well-established, quiet neighborhood and tried to buck the system.

In this stifling, controlling atmosphere, we children were expected to wear tight, long-sleeved shirts with every button fastened. Our entire bodies were to remain covered. Exposing any flesh was the height of worldliness. I felt that buttoning my shirt to the very top in the heat of the summer was beyond oppressive, and since there was seldom money for new clothes, my single shirt grew tighter as I grew older.

We also enjoyed little diversion in this border town. Once, to entertain ourselves, my brothers—Jerry, Johnny, and Allen—and I erected a crude basketball standard. We played basketball much of each day for a week, and then one evening three men from the "priesthood" demanded that we tear it down. They said it was too worldly; they didn't want other kids in Short Creek watching us waste our time playing basketball. The dismantling of the basketball standard didn't stifle our quest for fun. Next we proceeded to fix up an old motorcycle, and we rode it up and down the dirt streets for three days. Mysteriously, it disappeared one evening. Next, Johnny purchased a horse and challenged any of his fellow Short Creek neighbors to a race up and down the dirt street in front of our trailer. The following Sunday, Brother Hammond, one of the group's preachers, gave a castigating sermon about the influences of the corrupt world on the youth of the community. He spoke of shutting out the rest of the world, and of the evil influences of the LDS Church on the "true religion."

Regardless of all the claims that our way of life was supposed to draw families together, I had lost my mother for months at a time to the demands of providing a living for her children and her husband.

My neighbors back in Orem, who were members of the LDS Church, spoke proudly of their polygamist ancestors, even though the practice among them had long since ceased. I was old enough to observe that loving LDS fathers helped their sons erect basketball standards without ridicule or shame. No one in their community was demanding that the standards be torn down. I had often seen fathers and sons laughing as they played basketball together. I had never played a game of basketball with my father.

CHAPTER THREE

Mother's Christmas Prayer

Visiting the Governor's Mansion is a rare privilege when you're only nine years old. I was in the third grade and good friends with Governor J. Brackon Lee's son, Richard. My house was one block east of the mansion, and the school where Richard and I were classmates was four blocks to the west. I waited for Richard each morning outside the large glass doors of the mansion. Governor Lee often walked his son outside the big iron gates to send him off to school. Most every morning he would hand Richard a quarter while looking over his shoulder toward the mansion before distributing the coin. I had my suspicions that his wife didn't know about the exchange.

Richard and I were both pudgy little boys who enjoyed each other's company. As soon as our class work was completed, we would make a beeline for the little grocery store across from the school. Richard handed the clerk his quarter and asked for change. He always gave me one dime, keeping the remaining dime and nickel for himself. The year was 1952. My dime bought two Hostess cupcakes and a large bottle of Coke from one of those machines with the ice floating on top of the liquid. Richard bought three very large nickel candy bars. No matter what the weather, we sat on the front steps of the store and consumed our treasures. It would be fair to say that I have no idea what was learned in that third grade class, but somehow I can remember every bite of those cupcakes.

I wasn't really sure why the governor's son would even be seen with me, let alone share his allowance. I was a poor kid whose father had abandoned us. Around the Governor's Mansion, on the Avenues in Salt Lake City, are many very large, old brick homes that were built in the mid to late 1800s. At one time, they were the finest in the state of Utah, but by the 1950s, some of them were approaching the century mark. Suburbia had moved to the outlying communities of the valley. My mother sought refuge in one of these large homes to hide from the embarrassment and reality that my father had abandoned her.

One day while walking to school, Richard invited me to his house for dinner. That presented a huge problem because Mom didn't allow us to enter other people's homes without permission, and she never gave permission. Richard's invitation meant that I would be dining in the Governor's Mansion, if only I could find a way around Mom. If I agreed to go, the state police would have to do a background check on my family. That would be an even bigger problem because there were some definite skeletons in the Beagley closet. I asked Richard if there was any way he could sneak me in for dinner, and he agreed. I would just show up at six in the evening and ask to see Richard . . . Good plan!

The day came, and ten minutes before I was to leave for the Governor's Mansion, a stretch limo pulled up right in front of my house. Richard was running late from shopping in town and decided to drop by to pick me up. Evidently he had forgotten about our plan. Lady Luck was shining on both of us when the chauffeur knocked on the door. Mom was in the backyard with my two little brothers. I ran out of the house and climbed into the limo, demanding that we leave as swiftly as possible.

The handle that opened the front door to the mansion was nearly as big as I was. Richard introduced me to his parents. They were very polite and stately. The dining hall was as big as my entire three-story home. In a huge area in the middle of the hall stood a fifty-foot hardwood table. The butler announced that dinner was served. Richard and I sat at one end of the table, and the governor and his wife sat at the other. Richard said that his parents wanted to eat in peace without the disturbance of two giggling nine-year-olds. It would have taken a microphone and binoculars to carry on a conversation with his parents. The menu was roasted pork loin with some green mint jelly that was just awful. Fortunately, there were plenty of courses to choose from. Three different desserts supplied enough sugar to raise my triglyceride levels off the charts.

Once the ice was broken with the dinner invitation, I was cleared for further visits to play at the big house on a regular basis without a background check. We were assigned to stay within the children's quarters of the mansion. It was great seeing how the other half lived. Because it was early December, there were Christmas trees all over the Governor's Mansion. Richard had his very own tree in the children's play area. There were gobs of presents under his tree from all over the country, with his name on every one of them. Three weeks before Christmas, a huge crane set a sixty-foot blue spruce tree into the rotunda of the mansion. Over twenty workers proceeded to put the lights and decorations on the tree so that it could be illuminated that weekend. Richard and I watched between the spaces of the staircase spindles on the third floor as the little elves made the winter wonderland unfold. To me, it felt like magic.

The five youngest children in my family were very close to each other in age. Four of the five were boys, each spaced about fourteen months apart. Alan was the youngest of twelve and was very guarded by Mother. Johnny was the next youngest and was my paper route buddy. My sister Karen was squeezed between Jerry and me. Jerry was the boss of the younger children. We all marched to the rhythm of his drum. Jerry secured a paper route in our neighborhood. Johnny and I delivered the papers five evenings a week and early Sunday mornings. Jerry and Alan collected the money once a month. Johnny and I were young and stupid and thought that receiving one-half of the profits was a great deal. It wasn't until years later that we figured out we were doing most of the work for half the pay!

Although my mother struggled financially, she refused to accept aid from the state or the LDS Church. She couldn't leave the home for employment and still nurture her own children, so she chose the only field of labor with which she was familiar—she turned the bottom floor of our Avenues home into a day-care center for infants. Ten baby cribs were lined up in a row in the living room. Women from the community brought their children under the age of one to Mom for daytime care. She watched over the infants' every need with the loving hands of a mother of twelve. This situation presented many new challenges.

One snowy afternoon following school, after Richard and I had eaten our goodies and said good-bye, I walked around the corner from the Governor's Mansion and headed up the street. Even though the snowflakes were large, I could see several police cars and an ambulance with lights flashing in front of our house. I envisioned all sorts of horrible things. Was my mother dead, or one of my brothers seriously hurt? As I ran up the stairs and onto the front porch, I could see two paramedics carrying out a small body bag from the house.

The more questions I asked, the more stern looks I received. Finally, my older sister Karen told me that one of the infants whom my mother cared for had awakened from her nap and pulled down a plastic wrapping that covered articles of dry-cleaned clothing. The plastic surrounded the little girl's head, and she stopped breathing. Paramedics attempted to revive the child for over thirty minutes with no success. The little girl's mother had come to check on her child during the day and had hung the dry cleaning on the outside of the crib. The police determined that my mother was not at fault, but she always blamed herself for the little girl's death.

Mom was devastated. She had no husband to support her and no family members she could turn to for comfort. She refused to accept help from anyone as long as her two hands were able to work. Now it was Christmastime, and there was nothing to give to her children. After visiting the beautifully decorated Governor's Mansion, I wondered why there was no sign of Christmas in my home. No tree, no presents, no cards—nothing. The contrasting spirit between Richard's mansion and my home caused me to question the fairness in the Lord's distribution of wealth to us mortals. Christmas was so alive and beautiful in one place, yet so silent and absent at the other. Mother loved the yuletide season and had always used the occasion in the past to decorate our home and to buy needed clothing her children lacked.

Two days before Christmas, I stayed home from school with the flu. My bedroom was on the second floor just above the front porch, overlooking the street. I lay in bed for several hours in the morning burning up with a fever. Unable to stand the pain any longer, I crawled down the stairs to seek some motherly relief.

Mom's bedroom was at the foot of the stairs on the first floor. As I approached her door, I could hear her praying. Mom always prayed aloud, feeling it was the only way the Lord would hear her. I rested my ear on the doorjamb and listened to her prayer, which contained many tears and pleas for forgiveness and comfort in her behalf. Her petition to the Lord for help in providing a Christmas for her children was most sincere and humble. "Please, dear Lord, help my children have a Christmas." She was so alone and empty. Somehow my fever seemed of little importance. Quietly, I retraced my footsteps.

When Christmas Eve rolled around, I was still sick. I found great relief from the fever by placing my head on the cool bedroom window while watching as my brothers did their famous hooky-bobbin' in the new-fallen snow. There was a stop sign at the bottom of our block. They would hide in the bushes until a car came to a complete stop and then spring out and latch onto the back bumper. There wasn't another stop sign for six blocks, so we would get one heck of a ride. Most of the drivers knew they had acquired exterior passengers but didn't seem to mind. The Avenues are located on some very steep hills, so when our ride was completed we could just slide back home. It was good, cheap fun.

While enjoying the beautiful winter scene from my bedroom's elevated vantage point, I was surprised to see my mother walk out of the house. I watched as she pulled the torn coat that she had owned for years over her shoulders and turn toward town. She rarely left home, so my curiosity was high. Our only car was old and had been wrecked by my sixteen-year-old brother several weeks earlier. We had no money to fix it, so it sat beside our house looking all beat-up. Was it possible that Mom just wanted to be alone on Christmas Eve? I worried about her. It's very difficult to watch the one person you truly love suffer. Mom was my very anchor to life!

I was still perched on the cool window watching my brothers play in the snow two hours after Mom had left for town. In the dark of the night, I saw a taxi pull up and park in the middle of the street. There was too much snow on the driveway and curb to park anywhere else. I never expected to see Mom step out of the taxi, but she did. There was a very small Christmas tree tied to the top. The driver helped her unload the tree and a trunk full of boxes and sacks. Each of us children were rushed off to bed with threats of horrendous results if we didn't obey.

Mom's cure for the flu was Golden Seal tea and frozen green peas. It's no wonder the illness hung on so long with such potions for a remedy. Just before midnight, she came up the stairs to check on my condition. Sure enough, there was tea and more peas in her hands. I asked about the taxi and was told to go to sleep.

The next morning there were eight different stacks of clothing positioned around the living room. Mom thought that wrapping presents was a waste of time. At the bottom of my stack was a brand new pair of 501 Levis that had never been worn before, with the tags still on them. Next there was a pair of pajamas, followed by a new white T-shirt. Some nuts and an orange rested on top of the stack. The new Levis meant that I would be wearing my very own new pair of pants, not hand-me-downs, for the first time in several years.

After examining our Christmas treasures, we approached the kitchen to celebrate the occasion with a hardy breakfast. My sister Karen opened the cupboard doors to find that the only food item available was two packages of vanilla pudding. Mom had spent every penny of her grocery money on Christmas gifts. To a hungry nine-year-old, the cupboard truly looked bare. As I sat at the kitchen table staring out the window toward the Governor's Mansion, I wondered what elegant feast Richard was dining on in his mansion. I wanted to join him, but I knew that a visitor would be frowned upon on Christmas Day. Karen made some very lumpy vanilla pudding and we celebrated Christmas around the piano. The orange and nuts came in handy later on in the day. A partial smile returned to Mother's face as we sang the songs of Christ that day.

Being a member of a massive family, I had learned to speak only when spoken to. The tenth child of twelve carries little clout in the family pecking order. Even though I had heard Mom's prayer and had seen her leave the house on Christmas Eve, I said nothing to other family members about my discovery. Mom was from the old school of discipline. When we spoke out of turn, we often picked ourselves up off the floor. She was a large woman who had been raised with many rough brothers.

Even though I didn't have the courage to ask about the source of our Christmas goodies, I wondered for years where Mom found the money to buy all those things. I didn't find the courage to ask until I was twenty-one years old and the proper occasion to be alone with her presented itself.

I had been away from home for two years and cherished the opportunity to return to spend the Christmas season with my mother. As we sat on the porch of the nursing home, late into the evening, the ghosts of Christmas past returned. I spoke to my mother of the love and admiration I had for her. There never was a more hardworking, lovable person than my mother. I loved her with all my heart.

The time was right, and somehow I mustered up the courage to tell Mom about overhearing her prayer many years before. Her face turned red, and she slugged me on the shoulder, saying, "Oh, David, you weren't supposed to hear that!" There was silence for a time, and then Mom related a most beautiful story. She swore me to secrecy, a vow which I am now breaking more than a decade after her death.

As I remembered watching Mom leave the house on the Christmas Eve so many years before, the image of her tattered coat still loomed large in my mind. She refused to spend any money on herself; thus much of her clothing was very old. The coat she threw over her shoulders had a tear in the seam of the arm. Stuffing was falling out, and she looked somewhat indigent. I'm sure she realized her plight in life, but she refused to complain.

With the snowflakes falling and her coat in place, Mom walked two blocks to the south and turned toward town on South Temple Avenue. She recalled walking past the Governor's Mansion and admiring the beautiful Christmas lights. The two large retail stores in the 1950s were Kress Company and Woolworth's. Both were large buildings next to each other in the heart of Salt Lake City's Main Street. After turning the corner onto South Temple, Mom had another seven blocks to walk to reach the department stores. Knowing that it was Christmas Eve and having no money, she said that her plan was to contact the credit department of both stores and ask for a loan of $100 to purchase Christmas gifts for her children. Mom knew that Heavenly Father listened to her prayers, but now it was late on Christmas Eve, and she knew that she must take matters into her own hands or her children would miss Christmas. She couldn't let that happen.

Evening comes early in the Rocky Mountains. It was 5:30 and dark. The stores would be closing at 7 p.m., so Mom's steps were hurried. Her first approach was at Kress Company. The credit manager took one look at her sloppy attire and demanded that she leave. She attempted to explain her condition to the man, asking for his assistance. He promptly called for security, and she was escorted out of the building. (No wonder Mom didn't want anyone to know her story!) How humiliating that must have been for a proud woman such as my mother. With little hope for better results, she went next door to Woolworth's and pleaded her case to that store's credit manager. He was somewhat more sympathetic, but he also insisted that she leave.

It was one thing to be abandoned and left alone, but to see her children go without the necessities of life was more than Mom could bear. With tears beginning to flow, she started the trek back home empty handed. Three doors up from the large department stores was a savings and loan company. Mom pressed her nose against the glass window to detect any form of life. There was none, so she proceeded up the frigid street. From the corner of her eye she saw some movement in the back of the savings and loan office. Mom rushed back and proceeded to pound on the glass window. Now the meek beggar had turned into a desperate hen protecting her chicks. She was completely oblivious to the hundreds of shoppers passing by, watching the commotion. She had asked God for help, and she was going to do everything within her power to assist him in fulfilling his part of the bargain.

As the gentleman in the back of the savings and loan looked toward the street to discover the source of the disturbance, what a sight he must have seen. There stood an older lady with the lining falling out of her torn coat, beating on the window. The door was locked, and it was well after closing hours. He beckoned for her to go away, but the pounding continued. He walked to an adjoining room to escape Mom's glance, but she continued to knock. Finally, seeing that she would not go away, he entered the front office to get a closer look at his intruder. He didn't open the door, but spoke through the glass window. "What is it you want?" he asked. Now the tears were streaming down Mom's cheeks.

In the cold of that evening, Mom stood on the crowded sidewalk and shouted through the window, describing the condition of her family. She explained that her husband had left and that she had twelve children who would have no Christmas without some help. The questioning eyes of the gentleman on the other side of the glass filled with compassion, while he stared into my mother's desperate eyes. He recognized the anguish of a pleading woman. He motioned for her to walk to the door. Mother heard the lock open and the gentleman's sympathetic arms found her a seat. While recalling the story, Mother said that never had a warm chair felt so soothing. The gentleman asked her to wait while he returned to his desk. Soon he emerged with an envelope in his hand. He explained to Mom that the $100 bill inside was to be a present to his wife, but she had already received several Christmas presents and knew nothing of the money. He leaned down and kissed my mother on the forehead and wished her a Merry Christmas. He insisted that the money wasn't a loan, but a gift.

Mom returned her appreciation and rushed next door to one of the very same stores where she had been asked to leave shortly before to purchase the Christmas presents for her children. She beat the closing doors by only five minutes. Before he allowed her to fill the shopping cart, the manager insisted on seeing her money to purchase the articles of clothing. Proudly, Mom produced a crisp, new $100 bill.

Following that Christmas on the Avenues, we moved once again. Years later, Mom returned to the building where the savings and loan had been located, only to find that another business occupied it. She had forgotten to ask the gentleman's name, nor did he offer. Somehow, I think that was the way he wanted it.

The reason for breaking my oath of secrecy to my mother now involves a deep longing from within to thank a stranger whom I have never met for allowing me to experience the love of Christmas so many years ago. A loving God in Heaven surely hears and answers a mother's prayers. Now that I am approaching sixty years old, the possibility that the giver has left this life is very high. If he is departed, undoubtedly he has received his rewards from the Giver of all gifts. However, I wish to let it be known that there has never been a Christmas come and go that I didn't fall to my knees and thank God for a man who must have recognized the love of Christ through my mother's pleading eyes.

Each Christmas, because of the generosity of a stranger, my sweetheart and I, along with our six children, have attempted to seek out a needy family and anonymously supply their needs. Our Christmas Eves are filled with fond memories of scrambling from doorsteps to avoid detection. Christmas is a magical time that allows the redistribution of God's wealth. It is the one time each year when each of us who have been blessed with a shiny new quarter can cash it in and share at least one dime with those who have nothing. The giving process seems to perpetuate itself when the giver remains anonymous. Somehow, I believe that's the way he wants it!

Someday, I will have the privilege of knowing the name of the giver and of sharing his embrace. But for now, whoever you are, present or departed, please accept a sincere thank you!

CHAPTER FOUR

Down on the Farm

Now that Dad was illegally married to more than one woman and Mom had accepted his demands, fear of the law's retribution necessitated Mother's having to move the family often. We rarely stayed in one home for more than two years. When I was nine, and a third grader, we sold our home in the Avenues of Salt Lake City and Mother began searching for a new location, one that was less visible to authorities and beyond the suspicions of neighbors. Since Dad had become quite vocal in declaring his right to marry whom he wished, we lived in constant fear that his openly arrogant attitude was sure to summon the sheriff, who would haul all of us off to jail. Mom scanned the entire state for a place where we would have no neighbors.

At length, she located an old farm in Wellington, Carbon County, Utah. The move would require that Mom and the older brothers run the farm, since Dad wasn't anywhere to be found when it was time to do work. He was insistent, however, that the farm produce the same amount of money each month as had the day-care center. In order to accomplish that task, each one of us would have to work from sunrise to sunset. As an added benefit to him, isolating his first family in a remote community some two hours away would allow Dad the freedom to "do his thing" unobserved.

The soil in Carbon County is mostly clay. On a good year, achieving even a meager crop is challenging. Even tumble weeds refuse to grow in Carbon County. The farm that Mom had selected in Wellington had no neighbors for several miles. The ground was hard and unyielding to any-thing but sugar beets. The thought of applying a hoe to such rock-hard clay in order to thin or weed sugar beets always caused shivers to run down my spine. My memories of Carbon County were also dark. The area is filled with gullies and clouds of dust.

My metamorphosis from city kid to farm boy was, to put it mildly, a shock. Mornings began with my older brothers dragging me out of bed at 5:30. Chores included feeding the horses and chickens, then milking the cows and separating the cream with a belt running from our old John Deer tractor. At 7:00 a.m. we would take a break for breakfast, followed by a march to the sugar beet fields, armed with hoes to weed and thin the plants. The rows were long and the summer sun was hot. Sometimes as we started down a new row, I would pause to straighten and stretch my aching back. Then I would remove my hat, wipe my forehead on the sleeve of my shirt, and scan the field for an unseen distant goal.

With blistered hands and weary legs, I worked as hard as a nine-year old could, but I always lagged behind my older, stronger brothers. Mercy only came from Jerry, who often slipped over to my row to help me catch up. But I would hear about my slacking as the day wore on. Once, I pulled the "collapsing" trick, falling into the dirt and complaining that I was too little for this kind of work. My older brother Larry didn't buy into it. He picked me up off the ground and firmly corrected my attitude. Thereafter, fear of Larry was much more intense than the pain from my blistered hands!

Sometimes, when my brothers were far ahead and couldn't see me, I would sneak away and sit in the cool water of the irrigation ditch. One hot summer day, while we were working in the beet fields, one of my broth-ers yelled for us to look down the road. I stood erect and hooded my eyes with a hand. I was tired and sweat rolled off my face. In the distance, I saw a cloud of dust rising. That usually meant that our sister Karen was bringing us cool water to drink. We all dropped our hoes and ran to the edge of the road. But when the dust settled, we saw that the vehicle was not our old farm truck and its driver was not my sister. This car was new and shiny, a top-of-the line, yellow and black 1953 Mercury. Out popped Dad, grinning from ear to ear. He had talked Mom into purchasing him a new car so that he could travel more easily between his multiple wives and many children that were scattered across the state. Of course, Dad was unemployed. His only occupation was propagating, and yet he had the audacity to flash his new car at those who were doing backbreaking work to pay for it. Each of us turned away from him without uttering a word and slowly walked back to the beets.

Perhaps it isn't right to hate one's own father, but that day in the sugar beet fields, as the anger welled up inside me, I came close.

On another occasion, Mom excitedly gathered us children around the dinner table to announce that she had received a letter from Dad. Because the mailbox was constantly empty, she wanted us to experience reading the letter together. After we surrounded the table, she carefully opened the letter and began reading the contents. What had been a pleasant smile on her face turned to a look of horror. She dropped the letter and ran to her bedroom. None of us knew what to do. Should we open the bedroom door and attempt to soothe Mom, or should we read the contents of the letter with fear of her reprisal? Finally, Larry picked up the letter from the floor and began reading it silently. His face became red.

"What does it say?" shouted Jerry.

There was no reply. Several days later, Jerry told us younger children that the letter announced that Dad had married another woman and was asking for Mother's permission after the fact. So much for Mom's privileges of being the first wife.

CHAPTER FIVE

Step to the Rear of the Bus

In spite of all our hard efforts, the farm failed miserably. Mom was forced again to move her family back to the Orem neighborhood that had given her so much embarrassment and ridicule. She converted her home that had housed a day-care center for little children into a full-time nursing home for elderly ladies. That left no room for her own children! We had to move ten blocks away into a rented house. When our summers in Short Creek ended, we would return to our Utah County home and enroll in school there. The leadership of the polygamist movement would have preferred that all their followers school their children in Short Creek, but their buildings were small and would not accommodate the enrollment of the several hundred members who migrated back and forth between Short Creek and Salt Lake City or Utah County.

Thus I spent my years between the ages of nine and fourteen comparing the two different cultures. In Short Creek I was taught that my classmates in Orem were evil and destructive and that my summer friends had all of life's answers. I watched this southern Utah community desperately attempt and fail to develop a "Zion community." Short Creek was so primitive and undeveloped that many of the Salt Lake and Utah County fundamentalists refused to even visit the community, "until they cleaned it up."

Though I was young, I knew that my life demanded more parental acceptance and nurturing. I wondered, if these LDS families in Orem are supposed to be so bad, how do they appear to possess so much love and family unity? How could my father, who insists on living a "higher law," refuse to acknowledge me as his son and love me?

The bud of hope is fragile. It can be nurtured or destroyed by those who tread near its seed bed. A kindness can urge it to blossom; a displaced remark can cause it to wither. Now, at age fourteen, I felt the stirring of hope for my long-sought-after dream of happiness in the person of Janet Yearsley.

The Yearsley family lived across the street from our rented home in Orem. Janet was one of the most beautiful girls I had ever seen. Even though I was shy and fourteen, my hormones were in full function. Janet and I rode on the same bus to and from Lincoln Junior High. I always sat alone in the rear with my long-sleeved shirt buttoned up to my chin. In an effort to protect my parents, I had been taught not to speak about my family with classmates, although it was common knowledge that we were polygamists. Remarkably, the other kids usually left me alone. From my vantage point on the bus's bumpy back seat, I could quietly spend eighteen minutes—nine each way—observing Janet, her beauty, and her grace. Often I would fantasize that she would come down the aisle and ask to sit by me. She was a cheerleader, popular, and full of life. I was smitten, but I dared not say a word to her.

One day, to my absolute astonishment, Janet walked past her friends at the front of the bus and moved toward me in the rear. I froze. Was this real or was it my mind playing tricks on me? I quickly shifted my gaze out the window to avoid eye contact. My hands became clammy and my lips grew dry. Suddenly, she was standing right in front of me. I continued to stare out the window.

"Do you mind if I sit here?" she asked.

I swallowed hard and forced myself to glance up at her. She had the face of an angel. My oath to be economical with words had not fashioned me to be a great communicator, let alone carry on a normal greeting to a fellow classmate. I had a hard enough time talking with boys my age. But what about the most beautiful girl in the school? I cleared my throat. My fourteen-year-old voice had a tendency to crack, so I attempted to summon a low, manly tone. "Sure," I said.

Janet smiled. My mind went blank and once again I turned my head to stare out the window. Suddenly I felt the bench relax as she settled in beside me. I could hear the rustle of her dress; I smelled her sweet perfume. My senses were bombarded with information that I had never before processed. Janet was the first to break the ice.

"Do you play sports?" she asked.

I half turned toward her and shook my head.

"You come from a big family, don't you?" she asked. "How many brothers and sisters?"

I had been trained to look for hidden meanings in all questions about my family that were asked by "outsiders." To her casual inquiries, I answered with short replies since my first suspicion was that she might be gathering information to use against my parents. I wondered if perhaps her parents had assigned her this humanitarian act so that they could confirm suspicions about our family. But, within a few minutes, I began to realize that Janet was genuinely interested in me, and I sensed in her no prejudice or judgment. I reasoned that her visit to the rear of the bus was a one-time occurrence, but time would prove me wrong. She was doing what she did best: developing a new friendship.

After that, we sat together as she spoke of her family and her church. I listened carefully to every word as she spoke, especially about her loving mother and father, who were an integral part of her life.

On one occasion, as the bus slowed to our stop, she asked, "Would you like to come over to my house on Friday evening?"

My heart began to race. "Maybe," I said, forcing out the words. Then a shock of fear shot through me, and I added, "If I can . . . I mean, I'll have to see."

The door to the bus flew open and a few students stood up to leave. Janet gathered her books and turned to me and smiled. "I'll be looking forward to Friday."

I was vague with my commitment. Janet's invitation was wrought with many problems for me. If my family caught me associating with "the world," especially the female world, I could be banished to Short Creek, and not just for the summer. There, my older brothers would make sure that I stayed busy enough never to venture away from home again. Furthermore, visiting Janet would be interpreted as a definitive sign of rebellion. If I were to meet her, my only option would be to go to her home in secret.

Suddenly, an element of fear permeated my mind. I had been told many stories about the strange things that happened in outsiders' homes. We were not permitted to enter any of their homes or trust their words. "Your neighbors are just looking for any opportunity to turn us in, or even worse, convert us to their religion," I was constantly told.

The possibility that I lived in a neighborhood filled with caring, normal families was foreign and frightening to me.

As much as I was scared by Janet's invitation, I was also intrigued. As I stepped from the bus and walked down the street toward my home, I found myself devising a plan and weighing the consequences. "My mother is away working all day," I mused. "My older brothers and sisters also work and nobody ever keeps track of me. I could easily slip over to Janet's house and no one would ever know the difference."

My mind continued to work on the problem. What would I wear? My entire wardrobe consisted of one pair of pants and two hand-me-down shirts. One shirt was always in the laundry while I wore the other. And that presented another dilemma: I might not even be able to wear the clean shirt! The rule among my four brothers and me was: "He who gets to the shirt first gets to wear it." The five of us were spaced about sixteen months apart and shared a single bedroom. We were all similar in size. A friendly rivalry for a clean shirt was ever present, and I often came up on the short end.

I didn't own a toothbrush, so I would need to find a quarter to buy one. My older brother owned some underarm deodorant. I could swipe some of that. He also had a bottle of *Elsha* cologne. Sneaking a splash of that would endanger my life, but I determined to chance it. I eventually decided that visiting Janet was worth the risk. I took to the task of carefully hand-washing my best shirt the night before and then hiding it from my brothers so it would be mine the next evening.

That Friday, after school, I waited for all my siblings to leave the house. Then I retrieved the shirt and ironed it so that it looked crisp and beautiful. I brushed my teeth—for the first time—and dabbed a little *Elsha* behind both ears.

The distance between our house and the Yearsleys' was a few paces, but it seemed like one of the longest treks of my life. After checking to see if the coast was clear, I scampered across the street and sidled up to a tree, as if to become invisible. I could feel my heart pounding in my chest. "Just breathe normally," I said to myself. I turned toward Janet's doorstep and measured the span in my mind. I looked back at my house. Convinced that I had not been seen, I composed myself and made my way to the Yearsleys' porch. I smoothed my shirt and reached for the doorbell. Then I froze. What I was doing was in open defiance of my parents' orders. All former arguments that I had with myself shot through my brain. Was

I committed to this course of action? I did not want to disappoint my mother, but I needed to satisfy my quest for happiness and normalcy. I squeezed my eyes shut and reached out a finger to the doorbell. The melody reverberated throughout the house. There was no turning back now. I prayed fervently that someone would answer the door quickly so that my family wouldn't see me standing on the porch.

Feeling great relief, I soon heard footsteps coming toward the door and I detected the latch moving. In an instant Janet's mother was framed before me in the open doorway. With a big smile, she grabbed my hand and shook it vigorously.

"David Beagley! So nice to finally meet you!" she gushed.

I felt my face grow hot. I looked down and mumbled, "Thank you."

She took me by the arm and ushered me into the house. "Come and sit in the living room," she said.

I obeyed.

Mrs. Yearsley was a nice looking, pleasant woman, outgoing, and ever in motion. Her smile put me at ease. She sat me down in front of a glass of milk and a plate of cookies—not store-bought cookies, but fresh, homemade cookies!

"Help yourself," she said as she turned toward the kitchen. "Janet will be down in a minute."

If I gasped, she didn't let on that she had heard. I just sat there stunned, scanning my memory for a time when someone had done such a thoughtful thing for me. Then my upbringing kicked into gear. Suddenly suspicious, I surveyed the room, checking all around me for someone who might show up and eat my cookies. Having come from a large, poor family, I knew what it meant to spar for a share of the food. Satisfied that I was alone, I turned back to the feast and reached out a finger to touch the glass of milk. It was cold. My fingerprint produced a tiny drop of condensation that trickled down the side of the glass. A smile spread across my face. Cookies and milk. I still could not conceive of anyone doing something so kind for me.

Maybe the Yearsleys' don't know I'm from a polygamist family, I thought. My musings were abruptly broken by Janet bounding into the room.

"David! I'm so glad you decided to come!"

I started to stand to greet her but she motioned me to remain seated.

"Eat your cookies and drink your milk," she said.

"They're really for me?" I asked, incredulously.

"Yes," she said, half laughing, "And I expect you to eat all of them."

The thought crossed my mind, *What if I had decided to stay home?* How inconsiderate that would have been after I now saw the planning that Janet had put into making my visit pleasant. Suddenly at ease, I allowed myself to indulge in cookies and conversation. We laughed, we talked. I deftly maneuvered around her questions about my family, but Janet seemed more than happy to talk about her own family. When her parents later joined us, they spoke of their wonderful activities as a family, how they loved each other, how they were happy in each other's company. And they loved their church. Almost every sentence was filled with some reference to their religion. The more they talked and the more I listened, the more convinced I became that the Yearsleys possessed something that brought them considerable happiness. I was totally unprepared for the experience I was having. These "outsiders" had no apparent ulterior motive; there was nothing sinister going on in their home; the church they spoke about didn't appear to be the evil religion I had been warned about in those never-ending meetings in Short Creek. All the Yearsleys wanted to do was get to know me and feed me cookies. I felt a calm, sweet peace wash over my troubled soul. I felt accepted and longed to experience in my home the kind of love that the Yearsleys had in theirs.

When I stepped from their porch that evening, I felt something inside me trying to come alive. The bud of spiritual awakening wanted to grow; it needed to grow. Each time I entered the Yearsley home thereafter I felt the stirring of something special in the deep recesses of my soul. Call it hormones, call it warm cookies, call it the Spirit, I sensed a palpable feeling of goodness permeate their home. I felt warm and accepted. *Why is my family so bent on criticizing and avoiding these people?* I wondered. *Why can't they see in the Yearsleys the good neighbors that they are?*

Later, Janet invited me to go with her and her ward on a hay ride. By this time, I had become adept at sneaking out of my house to visit her. "It will be dark," I would reason. "No one will recognize me." I was still paranoid about being caught and the news being broadcast to my family. Janet and I sat on the back of the hay wagon away from others. Late that night, we exchanged a kiss and expressed our feelings for each other. To someone who had never been kissed, I received her affection like a parched desert receiving water. My feelings for Janet and envying the happy life she enjoyed began to blossom within me. One Sunday following my fifteenth birthday, after Mom left for work, I peered out through a crack in the curtains, watching for the Yearsleys to pile into their car and head off for church. When they were gone, I dressed in my clean shirt, and then checked the house to make sure I was alone. Satisfied, I left the house and walked the six-block distance to the ward building where the Yearsleys would be. They had no idea I was coming. What a surprise it would be! I arrived just as the meeting had begun. Peeking through a partially opened chapel door, I spotted Janet and her family. The bench where they were sitting was full, so I made my way to the back of the chapel and settled into a lone chair to listen and observe. *I would find out if my family's warnings about the Mormons were true,* I thought.

The only memory that I had of attending LDS Church meetings was of Primary and treats for kids. Now, as a teenager, I was actually sitting in one of their chapels, hearing what they had to say.

I listened to the bishop address the people. What he said felt good to me. Despite the repeated warnings from my parents, siblings, and fundamentalist leaders to never step inside one of their churches, I felt a spirit of peace that comforted and engulfed me. I observed families sitting together reverently, loving each other, content and happy. I heard sweet hymns of gratitude for the Savior and watched young men neatly dressed in white shirts and ties pass the sacrament to the congregation. I was impressed.

Then, just as my path to spiritual awakening was aligning toward a bright goal, it took a sharp turn backwards. The undoing began when some young men who had passed the sacrament finished their duty and came to sit down behind me. At first, their conversation was merely annoying and distracting. But as I tuned in to what they were saying, which drew my focus away from the speaker, I became aware that their comments were about my sloppy appearance and body odor. In audible whispers meant to be heard, they belittled my clothes and snickered at my looks. I hung my head and slumped down, wishing I could disappear.

The beautiful spirit that I had enjoyed had now fled. I just wanted to escape. Their barbed remarks were cruel, but I knew what they said was true. I was everything they described: a polygamist kid who had holes in his pants and a strange looking shirt buttoned to the top. I had never experienced such demeaning and personal insults. I had come to their church hoping for acceptance and to feel more of the spirit of the Yearsleys' home. And for twenty glorious minutes I had felt something special.

What kind of people would do this? I asked myself. I was embarrassed and confused. Where was the logic? How could the spirit of the Lord be so strongly felt in one instance and be so void in another? *If this religion is so great*, I thought, *why would these boys attack me? Maybe my parents are right!*

I walked home slowly that day. The following morning I sat with Janet on the bus.

"You look so dejected," she said. "What's wrong?"

I hesitated, but she urged me on.

"I attended your church yesterday," I began.

"You came? Why didn't you come and sit with us?"

"The bench looked full, so I sat in the back . . . Some boys sat behind me."

I struggled to form the words and Janet seemed to understand. An expression of pain swept over her face as I explained how the boys had ridiculed me. Her eyes became moist when I touched the holes in my pants and asked her if the smell of my body was repulsive to people around me. She just took my hand in both of hers and held it tightly until we left the bus. She didn't say anything. She didn't have to. I knew her feelings toward me hadn't changed, but mine were as confused as ever. What I had imagined to be a clearly marked path to God and happiness was now the tender plant of hope being trampled under careless feet. I would not reconcile this detour in my life for a very long time. For now, I resolved, I would never step inside an LDS chapel again.

* * *

Those who work farms often wax philosophical in an effort to define themselves and their lot in life. My older brothers, thinking they had coined something original, were wont to proudly announce: "Beagleys hoe to the end of the row," and "If a job's worth doing, it's worth doing well." As a youth I hated those sayings. But years later, as a missionary in Scotland, they served me well.

Unlike other missionaries, rising at an early hour was no problem for me. Working sixty hours a week? Why not seventy? I disciplined myself to commit the missionary discussions to memory, word for word, and I practiced them daily. When I was sick, I worked through it and the tracting went on. Even as a junior companion, I gained the reputation that no senior would want me as his companion because "Elder Beagley will work you to death."

Beyond wanting to be dedicated, I held to another purpose for my hard work. I had believed with all my heart that blessings would fall into place for my faithful service. I reasoned that happiness, that most elusive of all blessings for which I had sought since childhood, was within my grasp if I offered unwavering, dedicated service. My mission was my chance to finally break clear of my past, my wilderness, and stride confidently into my promised land—happiness. I imagined that I only had to work hard enough and I would achieve it. Now, alone and hurting on a train to California and a "sub-par" mission where "sickies" were banished, I felt betrayed, punished, confused.

Self-pity was alive and thriving within me. Suppertime aboard the train found me not only feeling more and more sorry for myself but very hungry. I shifted in my seat hoping the gnawing, empty feeling would subside, for I did not relish the idea of mingling with fellow passengers in the dining car. My missionary name tag would give me away and I would have to act the part. Hunger finally won out. I adjusted my tie, put on my suit coat, and straightened my name tag. It read, "Elder Beagley, North Scottish Mission." But I was headed to California. I forced a smile on my face and made my way down an aisle toward the dining car.

Stepping through the door of the dining car, I saw several tables lined with fresh white linen and elaborate silverware. The windows were open, revealing the less than spectacular evening landscape of Nevada. A pleasant-looking older gentleman in a black uniform and patent leather shoes tucked a menu under his arm and led me to a softly lit table. After handing me the large menu, he filled my glass with ice water and stepped away. I scanned the list. I had learned from my mother, in my few dining-out experiences, to order from the right side of the menu. By so doing, the "affordable" entrees could be located. A quick glance at the prices, however, told me I wouldn't be eating out tonight. I had boarded the train with only thirty-five dollars in my wallet, which had to last me for the next month. Even the least expensive meal would consume a great deal of that amount.

Two days without food, I thought. I folded up the menu, set it on the table, offered the waiter a lame excuse, then slipped out of the dining car and headed back to my seat. I took the glass of ice water with me.

I have often wondered how the Lord shapes our lives. Does he carve out challenges to fit our personalities, or does he simply use our unique difficulties to refine us? As I rode the train that night, hungry and discouraged, I wondered if I had agreed, before this earthly life, to my particular adversities. Did I willingly consent to be born into a dysfunctional family, or was it a roll of the dice? Was I knowledgeable then and accepting of my recent illness with its operations and the subsequent relocation to a new mission? I pressed the cool glass of water to my forehead, then drew it away and tried to look through it. Everything appeared misshapen, strange, and distorted, much like how I was viewing my world.

What had I done in this or a former life that merited this punishment?

If there was to be a silver lining, what was the Lord's timetable?

Would I ever know happiness?

CHAPTER SIX

The Escape Plan

When I was sixteen, I broke away from my family and polygamy and set out to forge a new life. For eight long years I had felt trapped and miserable. I had enjoyed no affinity to my parents' new religion, and by then I knew that what I was being taught by the fundamentalists was wrong. Although I had felt slighted by the boys in Janet Yearsley's ward, I was cautiously intrigued with the LDS religion. The memory of the feelings I had experienced in the Yearsley home had incrementally worked a change of attitude in me, and now I was gaining the courage to do what I had to do—escape!

For two years I had patiently watched for an opportunity. Patience was an attribute I had been forced to acquire as a reserved, rarely recognized member of a large family. But my patience was waning. My longing to be free had been preceded by months of misery. I often cried myself to sleep at night, an unmanly thing, my older brothers would say. So I wept alone in the cover of darkness.

Summer, I decided, was when I would run away from home. Mother may have guessed that I was contemplating something because she didn't ship me to Short Creek as usual, rather she sent me to Salt Lake City to work with three of my older brothers. They were directed to keep me busy and make the work difficult enough that I would have nothing else to distract me. I moved into a garage in back of my father's house. I never saw him, as he was constantly traveling between his many wives and families. I worked construction from 5:30 in the morning until dark.

Like an indentured servant, I was compelled to do the dirty jobs, such as carrying cement forms, digging, hauling mortar, and cleaning up. At night, I would collapse exhausted into bed, tired and sore. My life was not my own. I had to get away!

Although I knew my mother had placed me in this situation in an effort to control me, I harbored no ill will toward her. I never questioned her love, and I knew that my leaving would cause her pain. In fact, I would have bolted much earlier had I not fostered feelings of guilt. My love for my mother was the only tie that had held me to Utah, but now my shallow existence had become unbearable and hopeless.

The brother who was just older than me and next to me in age was Jerry. Just one year earlier, Jerry had run away to Las Vegas to marry his high school sweetheart, Pat. He was seventeen then, and Pat was sixteen. Unable to support themselves without Mom's financial connections, they moved back to Salt Lake, where Jerry worked alongside me. He wasn't thrilled about his return to the controlling influence of fundamentalism or the domination of our older brothers. Jerry was a rebel, as was I, and had already proven himself willing to forge a new path. That attitude gave me courage and formed a bond between us. We spent daytime working hours quietly trying to make sense of our family's madness. We spent nights planning our escape.

Distance became our goal—if we could put some miles between us and the rest of the family, we might be successful. Distance soon became defined as Flagstaff, Arizona. When our family had first embraced polygamy, my oldest brother, Jess, named after my father, left in a rage and threatened to shoot any member of the family who showed up on his doorstep. Flagstaff was where he eventually landed. Jerry was elected to contact Jess, but neither he nor I knew what to expect since Jess's hatred for Dad and his estrangement from the family had been so severe. The age difference between my oldest brother and me was wide. Mother gave birth to Jess when she was twenty years old. She gave birth to me when she was forty-one. She had two more children after my birth. Jess grew up in a home where Mother and the children attended church and worshiped together. He loved the Lord and the Church, but he despised my father for what he had done to the family. After Jess married and left Utah, he made no attempt to contact or befriend the younger members of the family. He was, however, the only family member who lived outside of Utah. Thus his location provided both Jerry and me a viable place for escape.

With a great deal of hesitation, Jerry made the call. A long, uncomfortable pause greeted him.

"Jerry? My brother, Jerry?" Jess asked.

"Yes. One and the same," replied Jerry.

"I haven't heard your voice since your were a small boy."

"I know. It's been a long time."

Pleasantries turned to purpose. I hung onto every word. Soon, Jerry hung up the phone and paced.

"What did he say?" I asked. "Will he take us in?"

"I don't know. I think so. He didn't exactly invite us." That wasn't the response that I had hoped for. Our escape would not be easy. Jerry, his wife, Pat, and I just stared at each other, the weight of our decision pressing down on us. What if we did manage to escape Utah and make it all the way to Flagstaff, only to find ourselves homeless? Could we choose another destination with no family ties and make a go of it? Was it worth the risk? It would take a few days of fervent prayer to answer that question. Truly, we would be placing our future in the Lord's hands. I was left to wonder, *Is God carving a path for us or blocking it? Are we angering him by defying our mother and her religion?*

The commandment to honor my father and mother now took on a difficult meaning and potential consequence. No matter how hard I tried, I couldn't muster up much honor for Dad. Honoring my mother, however, caused mountains of guilt and soul searching. After a few anxious days of reflection, we three agreed that we must venture out and place our trust in a mysterious God whom we barely knew.

A major deterrent for my not departing earlier was my inaccessibility to an automobile. Recently, when I had turned sixteen, Mom made a down payment on a 1951 Chevy Coupe for me to drive. Her gift had two conditions: first, I had to make the monthly payments, and second, I had to promise to remain faithful to our family's beliefs. Of course I would have promised anything for a car! Mom could not have known that I had long been planning a one-way exit from the principles she had sought to solidify in me. All I had needed was transportation. Suddenly, with the prospect of deliverance at hand, I found myself less and less able to focus on daily tasks.

The attribute of patience, in which I had prided myself, began to disintegrate. My sleep became fitful. Dreams of deserting my suffocating environment once and for all invaded my thoughts. I awoke each morning fidgeting, sweating, imagining that I would be found out. During the day, my musings migrated from pole to opposing pole: on the one hand, I swelled with absolute elation with the possibility of freedom; conversely, I felt sick with despair over what my flight would do to my mother.

But I was suffocating.

My prayers had recently heightened in urgency as they evolved from pleas for help to seeking assurance that my contemplated action was right. During these difficult days, I spent considerable time reading in the New Testament in an effort to emulate the efforts of Joseph Smith, the prophet who restored Jesus Christ's gospel to the earth in modern days. I knew that he had found the courage to separate himself from difficult circumstances by reading the book of James. After I read the book of Matthew, one scripture played over and over in my mind: "He that loveth father or mother more than me is not worthy of me. . . . And he that taketh not his cross, and followeth after me, is not worthy of me. He that findeth his life shall lose it: and he that loseth his life for my sake shall find it" (Matthew 10:37–39). I wanted to trust God enough to believe these words.

Happiness has to be out there somewhere, I thought. *It isn't here.*

I knew I had to leave those whom I was commanded to love in order to find happiness.

Jerry, Pat, and I made a pact to escape on the weekend of July 24th. With all the celebrations during Utah's Pioneer Day, we reasoned, we could simply disappear in the masses of people who would be attending parades, picnicking, and playing. We would use "camping for the weekend" as our cover so that we would have plenty of time to flee the state. Absolute secrecy, of course, was essential to our plan. If my older brothers were to find out, they would certainly employ physical punishment. That prospect was frightening to me and loomed as a real possibility. My primary concern, however, was my age. At sixteen, I was still lawfully subject to my parents' supervision, and either one of them could have me arrested for running away. I was fully cognizant of that fact, for it had been repeatedly drummed into my head. No one easily escapes the grip of polygamy.

CHAPTER SEVEN

"Please, Officer,
Don't Send Me Back Home!"

Jerry owned an old 1949 four-door Chevy. Between his car and mine, we reasoned, we could transport our possessions—which weren't many—to Arizona. I packed clothes, some of Jerry and Pat's household items, and the breakable things into my car. Then I helped Jerry fill his entire rear seat and trunk with clothing and furniture to the point of overflowing. Finally, we strapped a rocking chair on the back. When we were finished we had crammed everything we could into the two vehicles. We weren't coming back.

Late Friday afternoon, Jerry and Pat departed for Little Cottonwood Canyon. I headed for Provo Canyon. Our plan called for splitting the escape routes so that if one of us was discovered, the other could go on to Flagstaff alone. We would spend the night in the canyons and then rendezvous the next day at the city park in Springville, Utah, far enough away from our family that we would be safe from discovery.

The sun was just dipping into the orange horizon when I drove away from Salt Lake City for the last time. I didn't look back longingly. I didn't imagine I would miss it. I didn't try to take a mental picture of it in my mind. I just focused dead ahead and set my sights on the future. Partway up Provo Canyon, I located a secluded spot and set up camp. Parking the car off the road and behind trees and brush, I hoped it would not be noticed. I didn't even make a campfire; my whole intention was to become invisible to the outside world. When the hot July air turned cool, the shadows of evening settled down in the canyon like fog. I threw a blanket around my shoulders and waited for my body to grow tired. But I couldn't sleep. I was on high alert and anxious, certain that every crack of a twig was my brothers hunting me down to drag me back. Jerry, Pat, and I had earnestly prayed that if we were caught, we would receive divine protection so that we could continue on our journey. Now, I felt like an escaped convict on the run. I soon found out that my feelings had merit.

In Salt Lake, late that evening, one of my older brothers had driven to Jerry's house to borrow some tools. When he knocked, no one had answered, so he peered through a window and saw no furniture, no pictures on the walls, nothing. Suddenly, he realized that our "camping trip" was simply a cover for a getaway. He tore back to the family to alert them. The first person he told was my mother, who called everyone together to hunt for us. When that failed, Mom called the police, and they issued an all-points bulletin in Utah for my arrest.

As the first light of morning broke over the tops of the mountains, I was already sitting behind the wheel, ready to go. I checked my watch— 4:30. I started the car, turned on the lights, and pulled out on the canyon road. I was alone. In the colorless realm between day and night when all things look gray, I felt solemn and afraid. Nothing in my life had prepared me for this experience. I wanted to feel excited for the prospect of a new beginning, but I was scared. My eyes were sore from lack of sleep. My muscles were tense. I knew that at any turn in the road a policeman might be waiting to arrest me, and the Arizona border seemed so far away.

The park where I was to meet Jerry and Pat was located right in the middle of Springville. I carefully approached it at 5:00 a.m. Jerry and Pat had also suffered through a sleepless night and had finally abandoned their mountain campground several hours earlier. Jerry had fallen asleep on Pat's lap on a blanket spread out on the park lawn. Pat was keeping watch. When I spotted them, a feeling of relief swept over me. During the night I had allowed my imagination to wander unchecked. Maybe they had been arrested. Perhaps they had changed their minds and returned home. When I saw the rocking chair still strapped to their car, my fears fled and I knew they were as determined as I to go forward at all costs.

I drove by them slowly, reasoning that if I stopped, and the police were looking for me, I might attract attention. I tapped on the horn and continued down the street to find a place to wait for them on the outskirts of Springville. When they saw me, they waved, and I thought I was safe. But the sound of the car horn would prove to be my undoing.

Situated near the park behind the fire station was the Springville Police Station. My horn startled the officer on duty. When he peered out the window, he immediately recognized my vehicle from the all-points bulletin. He jumped in his patrol car and came after me with lights flashing. I began to shake; my mind raced. I couldn't outrun him. I couldn't hide. My stomach grew sick and a hard knot formed in its middle. I could see myself being handcuffed and hauled off to jail. When I pulled over and stopped, I bowed my head and said, "Help me, Lord. I'm in trouble."

"Out of the car! Hands up!" the officer ordered, his gun drawn. I stepped out with hands held high. The officer turned me toward the car and shoved me up against it.

"Hands on top of the car. Spread your legs."

Just then Jerry and Pat pulled up behind the patrol car. As Jerry reached for his door handle, the officer turned the gun on him and demanded that he stay put.

"Officer, let me explain," I begged.

"Shut up! Don't move."

He frisked me roughly, then spun me around to face him.

"There's a warrant out for your arrest, young man. I'm taking you to jail."

I felt my knees buckle. I tried to plead, but my mouth wouldn't form words. My heart was pounding so hard I thought I would pass out. Just at that moment of great distress, something remarkable happened. A sense of calm washed over me, and a quiet voice came into my mind saying, "Tell the officer your story."

I had never heard a voice in my mind. At first, I didn't understand the message. It was both words and a feeling, a kind of communication I had not experienced. "Tell the officer your story." The voice was pleasant and distinct, not something conjured from the frenzied mind of a boy about to be incarcerated. I looked up at the policeman, who was red-faced, lecturing me about the evils of being a runaway, but the soft voice in my head seemed to be speaking louder than his yelling.

"Tell him now!" the voice said.

I opened my mouth. My body shook from head to toe. I began to form words that were not in my mind. My tongue started working independently from my body.

43

"My parents are polygamists," I said. "My brother and I are leaving the state to join the LDS Church and start a new life. I don't care about anything except getting out of here. Please let me leave with my brother."

I was surprised to hear myself declare that I was going to join the LDS Church, but I was experiencing something extraordinary and dared not question it. I paused. The officer stared at me, and I tried to maintain the posture of sincerity.

"Are you telling the truth or are you lying?" the officer asked.

I cleared my throat and explained our escape plan. He raised an eyebrow and the voice came back into my mind saying, "Tell him about your father."

Once again words tumbled out of my mouth. "My dad has several wives. I never see him. He doesn't even know who I am."

The officer's face suddenly looked angry. When he shifted his weight, which was considerable, I thought he was going to hit me. My first instinct was to duck. Instead, he pounded his fist on the hood of my car and uttered a few choice words. He ranted about selfish fathers who abandon and don't support their children. Then he stopped and surveyed me for a long time. I stood absolutely still. Feeling uncomfortable from the scrutiny, I started to say something to support my cause, but he told me I had said enough and to keep my mouth shut. He paced, shook his head, and straightened. Glancing at Jerry and Pat, he beckoned them to leave their car and come to him.

"Where are you headed?" he asked.

"Flagstaff," Jerry said.

"Why?"

"Our parents are polygamists and we are trying to escape. It's like we are captives in our own family."

As the officer continued to question them, Jerry answered, recounting the same story. Finally, the officer's expression grew relaxed and he told us that his father had abandoned him at an early age. Then he turned and looked me squarely in the eyes.

"It means this much to you?" he asked.

"Yes," I said.

"Enough to lose your car?"

I shot him a questioning look.

"You heard me. And you need to know that I could lose my job for this. You have eight hours to get out of the state. After that, I'm reporting an abandoned car."

I swallowed hard.

"That's the deal?" I asked.

"That's the deal." He looked at his watch and tapped on its face. "Eight hours, starting now." Then he got in his car and drove away.

The three of us just stood on the side of the road dumbstruck, not fully appreciating what had just happened. Pat was the first to speak.

"We can only take the essentials," she said. "We haven't got a lot of time. Get your clothes, David. That's all you can take. Jerry and I will unload what we can to make room for you."

What few belongings I had to my name I abandoned along the road that morning. When Jerry and Pat had discarded many of their possessions, we piled into their car and set out for Flagstaff. I was leaving with only the clothes I could hold on my lap. But freedom, glorious freedom, was more important to me than any sacrifice of comfort or material things. I was leaving with nothing and yet with everything. I had prayed and something incredible had happened—a voice had guided me, speaking through me, softening a heart. The Lord knew the exact words to speak to the officer that would allow me to continue along my journey in search of happiness. God also knew me! What a discovery! At sixteen, I had experienced divine intervention as a direct response to my plea for help. I had learned a basic truth: when we are patiently trying to do our best to move along a path the Lord has set before us, he will not lead us over a cliff. Rather, he will gently guide us through the difficult times until we reach a convergence of roads that move us toward our own promised lands. Deliverance may not come in the manner we expect, but it will come.

And happiness? It now seemed only a state away. Was happiness possible without the nurturing hand of a mother who loved me dearly? Would I even find happiness in this life without a father who knew and loved me? Does any young man learn to function properly without the training and love of one or both of his parents? Perhaps I would discover the answers to my questions in another state!

CHAPTER EIGHT

Flagstaff—a City for Rebirth

Transporting a juvenile runaway across state lines is a punishable offense. If caught, Jerry and Pat could face jail time. Although we had the assurance of the officer that he would not turn us in, we made our way to the Arizona border nervously, keeping one eye focused on the rearview mirror. Only when we saw the "Welcome to Arizona" sign did we feel relief and begin to engage in some lighthearted conversation. But our mood grew serious again once we arrived in Flagstaff. We had no idea what to expect from our brother Jess. He had told the family that he never wanted to see them again, but he and Jerry had shared happy dialogue on the phone.

As we pulled into our older brother's driveway, Jerry called out, "Jess! How are you?"

Jess looked dumfounded when he saw us. He put down his rake and rubbed his hands on his pants. "Jerry?" he asked incredulously.

"Yes, it's me! And this is my wife, Pat."

Jess reached his hand through the window and shook Pat's hand. Then he focused his eyes on me.

"David Beagley," he said quietly. "You're all grown up—a man."

I felt my face grow red and a lump formed in my throat. I remembered how much I had wanted to develop a relationship with Jess and how I had missed him when he had left home. Seeing him now sent a wave of emotion through me. The combination of looking into his eyes, my lack of sleep, the frightening escape, and the near miss with the law brought me to the point of tears.

"Hi, Jess," I whispered. I bowed my head to compose myself. Jess looked down too, and everything went quiet for a moment.

Finally Jess said, "You must be hungry. Come in and get something to eat. Meet my family. We'll unload the car later."

Jess was a very self-assured person. He carried himself with an air of arrogance that endeared him to some and alienated him from others. His marriage was in constant conflict, which kept Jerry, Pat, and me on guard most of the time. He wanted to welcome us into his home, but his wife didn't want to "mix our laundry with theirs." Soon, he was working hard to help Jerry find a job and locate a small rental house where the three of us could live. Once we were settled, and within a month of our arrival, I enrolled in Flagstaff High School as a junior. I felt as though I was reborn.

Now that I was a state away, my parents could do little to force my return. That my mother had dared contact the police to issue an all-points bulletin was beyond being brave. My family lived in paranoia of any legal attention and tried to remain invisible to normal society. I knew they would not want to go out of their way to pursue me. There were too many skeletons in their closets. However, I had no desire to hurt my mother or cause her to worry. Within weeks of my arrival, I summoned the courage to write her and put her mind at ease. Soon, this wonderful woman sent me good wishes and one hundred dollars for my school expenses. That opened a channel of communication that kept us connected for years. The remainder of my Utah family chose to disinherit me. I had rejected their religion, so they would in turn reject me until I "saw the light" and returned to the fold. As time went by, a few of my brothers and sisters softened, but most showed no tolerance.

Summer turned to fall. I entered my junior year with no secrets, no family to protect, no stigma of being a polygamist. I enrolled in an early-morning seminary class that allowed me to become acquainted with other LDS youth my own age from the two Flagstaff wards. I treasured these relationships. Saturday nights were filled with stake dances. I took advantage of every opportunity to attend firesides, Church outings, and parties at members' homes. I had never experienced socializing with teenagers my own age. I was like a child just being introduced to chocolate; I couldn't get enough.

My appreciation for Jerry and Pat grew as we settled into our new Flagstaff life and made of ourselves a family. They had risked their own safety to help me escape the bondage of fundamentalism and had taken me into their home to live. I felt greatly indebted to them. More remarkable, they had displayed this degree of caring when Jerry was only eighteen and Pat had just turned seventeen. Jerry extended to me a friendship that few people experience in a lifetime. Pat treated me with consummate respect. Together, they fed me, endured my teenage moods, and created an atmosphere of stability and loyalty in a home filled with love.

Several LDS families took a special interest in me and practically adopted me as their son. Gary and Ann Harenberg and their four children lived next door and made sure I was never hungry. Gary even taught me some choice Navajo words.

Gus and Ruth Palmer—Mom and Dad Palmer—made their home mine. I spent many Sunday evenings in their company. They could not have known how I watched their every move in an attempt to mirror their normalcy.

It was as though I had come to Flagstaff as a foreigner and was trying to learn a new culture. One Sunday night, when I was still trying to foster a normal life, I witnessed something that amazed me. We had just finished dinner and had retired to the Palmers' front room when their youngest daughter, Marena, said good night to the family. She walked over to her father and mother and kissed them. *I can handle that*, I thought. *Girls do that kind of thing.* But then, to my shock, six-foot-three, fifteen-year-old Mel stood up to say good night. I thought, *Surely he won't kiss his parents. He's a boy.* But I about fell off my chair when Mel leaned down and kissed his father right on the lips! He said, "Good night, Dad, I love you." I couldn't believe it! A physical and an audible expression of affection between two men? I turned my head away thinking that I was intruding on something very private. I could never have imagined such a thing. When the eldest brother, Tom, repeated the exact same action, I was embarrassed and confused. *Is this natural?* I wondered. *Do regular families express their love like this?*

It all seemed so strange. I had no point of reference. For days I struggled to understand what I had observed in the Palmer home. I was astonished and envious at how unashamedly the love between a father and his son was expressed. It was new to me. I wanted what they had, and it was from their example that the old yearning for happiness welled up inside me and bade my quest for it to continue. My escape from polygamy was one significant marker along what had been, and would be, a long journey to that goal.

I was beginning to realize that this happiness that I searched for had to include my having some kind of a father. If my earthly father was unavailable, then I must find another. The void that exists in a son's heart when his mortal father abandons him can only be filled in one of two ways: either finding someone else, an adopted father figure, or accepting Heavenly Father in the dual role of earthly and eternal parent. Could I trust another man to love me the way Brother Palmer loved his children, or should I take the big step and look toward heaven to fill the void in my life?

As I stared out of the window of the train bound for California, I thought about that question. I was alone in the dark, feeling little discernible happiness. My stomach was empty and my mind ached from too many questions: Did God hear me, see me, know me? Did he know what I was going through? Or was he somewhere else, solving bigger problems such as starvation in Africa, war, or some domestic abuse? Was my problem significant enough to warrant his attention? Did he understand the irony of my situation?—being called to serve as a missionary only to become unable to serve, then being exiled from Scotland to California. Did he realize that I was heartbroken and confused, that I could turn to no one but him for answers? Why wasn't he responding? That I had heard a voice in Springville which softened the heart of a rough cop was true, and there was no denying it, but now it seemed so distant and far away.

Mentally drained, I eyed the train's sleeper car and considered the comfortable bed that awaited me there. But the vibration of the train's wheels on steel rails had lulled me into a state of comfort, so I wadded up my suit coat for a pillow and curled up on my seat. Maybe I could rest, I thought. Maybe answers would come during the quiet of the night.

My thoughts drifted back to teaching the people of Scotland about the gospel of Jesus Christ, how families can achieve greater happiness here in this life by abiding by its principles and how they can remain together in the eternal world to come. I had become a keen observer of those principles in Flagstaff, for the families whose homes I frequented incorporated gospel teachings as a way of life.

Those families became my measuring stick for developing new behaviors. To see fathers, mothers, and children express love freely for each other provided me a sweet perspective on life. Their homes were filled with laughter and excitement. They had no secret lives or agendas. Fathers and sons enjoyed each other's company, a concept that was almost inconceivable to me. I observed no oppression, no unreasonable demands, no servitude. My Flagstaff friends refused to criticize their parents or belittle them publicly. Furthermore, the Flagstaff Second Ward was kind and accepting of us "Beagley transplants" from Utah. When Sundays came, so did the dinner invitations.

Frank and Louise Cosseboom's home was another in which I often found myself. Their daughter Patty made me want to be there. My spare time became Patty's time, and she didn't seem to mind. As was the case with all the families that had befriended me, the Cossebooms allowed me plenty of latitude.

During my childhood, the secrecy of polygamy had taught me to mistrust people, to be skeptical of others' intentions, and to shy away from affection. Even though I was out of polygamy's grasp, I tended to stand apart from the crowd, automatically suspicious, left to wonder if I could ever develop the attitude of trust and truly let people into my heart. I was quick to cover my feelings with sarcasm, discounted praise, and was instinctively averse to demonstrations of emotion. Sarcasm is the breeding ground for mistrust. He who dispenses sarcasm feeds his own ego with supposed humor while the recipient is left to wonder about his standing in their relationship. The inverted quotation of Proverbs 22:6 best described my Flagstaff incubation: "Train up a child in the way he shouldn't go; and when he is old, he will have a tough time departing from it!"

All told, my past clung to me like a shadow, and for the three years that I spent in Flagstaff observing people and sifting information, I wondered if the monsters of my youth would ever depart completely.

Patty Cosseboom entered my life as an answer to prayer. In her I discovered a model for trust. Suddenly, I had hope that I could conquer my character flaws and learn to trust completely. Patty allowed me to work through skeptical moments, one at a time, and was patient when I grew quiet. She and I knew that if I was backed into a corner, I would revert to sarcasm as a defense. She allowed me to be sarcastic with others, but she refused to tolerate it in our relationship. She demanded that our conversations be filled with meaningful, heartfelt realism. She was genuinely interested in me—a backwards, shy boy who had just purchased his first short-sleeved shirt. We became best friends. We fell in love, as teenagers often do, in a fun, exciting, and sharing way. Gradually, she taught me to converse with others my age in a positive manner. I sensed that she would never hurt me, and she seemed to know that what I needed most from her was her love, not her judgment. For two-and-a-half years, Patty tutored me through her example and created a foundation on which I was able to build other healthy relationships of trust.

By the time I turned eighteen, I was thrilled with the teachings of the Church. The skeptical part of me was giving way to the converted man, and I was allowing myself to consider a mission. But it wasn't an easy decision. Two years of my life seemed like eternity. Of course, I loved the Church, but I also loved the freedom I had known since I had moved to Flagstaff. A mission meant no schooling and no involvement with Patty. She had become my anchor, and I had come to depend on her for future happiness. I was afraid of being separated from her and left to ride the rough waters of life alone.

And so progressed my nineteenth year, vacillating, as prospective missionaries will, from one extreme to another.

On one occasion, I tested the waters of doubt by whispering to Patty that I wasn't sure I wanted to serve a mission. I had often spoken of going—and I really was planning to serve—but I wanted to see her response. She met my comment with silence for the rest of the evening. When I walked her to her front door, she looked me straight in the eye and said, "David, whether or not you go on a mission is your decision, but I'm going to marry a returned missionary!"

That night, I made my final decision to go on a mission. If a returned missionary was what Patty wanted, then that's what she would get. It was a time in my life when few opinions mattered to me except Patty's. If for no other reason, the Lord had put her in my path to introduce me to trust, the highest manifestation of love, and to set my feet firmly on the foundation of service and sacrifice. She said she was going to marry a returned missionary. It wasn't an option in her mind. She was willing to sacrifice for that kind of relationship. Was I? If she had said, "It's your choice, I'll support you either way," I don't know if I would have been strong enough to make the proper decision.

Late that summer, Patty left Flagstaff to attend Brigham Young University. Ironically, she had gone away to attend school in my hometown, and I was left alone in hers. Suddenly, I was all by myself and would have to stand on my own two feet. If I was going to build relationships of trust, I would have to use the training she had given me and do it on my own. If I was going to remain active in the Church and gain a stronger testimony, I would have to make the right choices. If I was going to serve a mission, I would have to go after it with all my heart.

CHAPTER NINE

The Blessings of Tough Love

I curled up on the seat of the train and tried to rest, but I still ached from my recent surgeries. The doctor had pronounced me "well enough," and the Church authorities said that was good enough for them. So, having convalesced enough to have satisfied everyone but myself, I had packed my mission clothes in an old suitcase, stuffed thirty-five dollars in my pocket, and boarded the train for California.

How time changes things, I thought. Only four years ago, I had barely escaped to Flagstaff. My own mother had called the police to catch and incarcerate me. Later, we had made amends and established a loving, long-distance relationship. When I graduated from high school in Flagstaff, she drove the entire stretch in her Volkswagen Bug to be with me. She beamed through the whole ceremony. Later, as I made plans for a mission, she told me she was proud of the stand that I had taken in joining the Church. I believed that she still had a testimony of the truthfulness of the Church, but she had made a decision to leave it, thinking that she could preserve her family. Ultimately, she could do very little to change the situation that Dad had forced upon her and us children.

One event that had changed my life, but seemed of little importance at the time, was receiving my patriarchal blessing. I had heard my friends talk about receiving their blessings, but I had no idea what they were talking about. Patty's parents suggested that I ask my bishop for a recommend, and I complied with their suggestion.

The stake patriarch lived in a neighboring town, so I knew very little about him. The idea that someone could lay his hands on my head and pronounce prophetic declarations about my life was almost beyond my imagination. What would such a person be like? I formed an image in my mind of this man of God, someone who could look into my very soul and reveal the mind of the Lord for my destiny. I arrived at his home alone on the appointed Sunday evening and knocked on the door. When he answered, he shook my hand and promptly called me by the wrong name. I was devastated. Instantly, the recollection of my father forgetting my name when I was young flashed through my mind. I suddenly felt out of place, and my old nemesis—skepticism—reared its ugly head. *Maybe getting a blessing from this forgetful old man isn't such a good idea,* I thought.

But I stayed to see it through. He asked me questions about my life— searching, caring questions. Slowly, my first impressions of this gentle man gave way to feelings of serenity. I decided I could give myself to his charge and allow him to deliver me a blueprint for my life. He asked me to pray and invite the Spirit to attend us. Then he positioned himself behind me, paused as if to collect his thoughts, placed his hands tenderly upon my head, and uttered words that I could have never imagined. For the second time in my life, I received the profound assurance that God knew me. He knew where I had been, where I was now, and what path I should take in my life. The patriarch stood in his prophetic calling, looked into my heart, and said, "Prophets of the Lord shall dine at your table . . . You shall be called to be a missionary and serve in foreign lands. Those whom you teach shall feel of your testimony and know that you are a man of God."

Now, as I lay resting on the seat of the train, I considered the patriarch's words—foreign lands. Surely it had been so. Scotland was where I had been called. But it hadn't lasted. Now California? Did that qualify as a foreign land? My skeptical mind began to discount my patriarchal blessing and its promises. Like dominoes, the promises began to fall faster than I could stop them. I sat upright as if to slap myself in the face, and thought, *Just because I don't understand, am I willing to throw away all that I believe and have sacrificed for?*

I stood, paced, and shook my head in disgust for my weakness. Regardless of the location of my mission, I knew that even now I was willing to sacrifice everything to continue to serve. But it hadn't started out that way.

Two months before my nineteenth birthday, I had filled out my papers to apply to be a missionary. I felt I was ready to serve the Lord. For almost a year, I had saved enough money to go. Finally, Bishop Hatch invited me into his office for an interview, which I considered a mere formality. He was very direct. He didn't care what I had been through; he only cared about my worthiness now. He asked me pointed questions. Was I keeping the commandments? I answered yes to each inquiry until he came to the issue of tithing.

Church members pay 10 percent of their income as tithing. It was a discipline I had not fully practiced. Because I was saving for a mission, I felt that tithing could slide a little—the money earned would be dedicated to the Lord's service, after all. Perhaps I had not paid it due to a lack of faith, or from fear or laziness. No matter how I had done the math, I figured that ten minus one should equal nine, but never eleven or fifteen or ninety-nine as I had heard "testifiers" claim. When I stumbled on the bishop's question of tithing, I told him I had enough money in the bank to make a lump-sum payment and catch up the whole year. He refused. It was the "practice" of tithing he wanted me to master and that would take time. Six months! My mission was to be delayed for half a year as I was to learn the discipline and blessings of regularly paying tithing.

I left his office feeling harshly judged. Others, less worthy in my opinion, were receiving their mission calls. Why was I being singled out? My pride was hurt. Why six months? Why not make me wait one month, or two? Why wouldn't the bishop allow me to pay the whole amount right on the spot? It was just money, wasn't it? Didn't he understand the sacrifices I had made in giving up my family to join the Church? Didn't he know my desire to serve a mission? He wouldn't waver.

Having been mistreated by a father figure pushed emotional buttons within me that I had only occasionally allowed to surface publicly. Now anger and criticism welled up inside me as I felt unappreciated by another male figure—Bishop Hatch. Fairness? What a joke! Where was mercy? I only felt the heavy hand of justice crushing me. My inclination was to throw in the towel. I'd show the bishop. If the Church didn't need me, then I certainly didn't need it! He was forcing me to be good. Where was the Christianity in that?

Eventually, however, after all the venting and self-pity, I had to admit that I had a testimony that the Church was true. How could I acknowledge my feelings and claim that they had no merit? I had seen what abandoning the truth could do to people. My own family had been shattered by a father that had looked straight into the sun and denied it. If I retreated now, what would my life be worth? Once more, I would become a captive, but this time I couldn't run across a state line to escape—I would be my own prison. So I returned to what I knew to be true by asking myself, "What do I believe and how deeply do I believe it?" I decided that I would submit to the bishop's counsel, and beyond that, I would do all that he had asked of me. I would not accept well-wishers' pity for my situation or allow them to engage me in criticism of the bishop. I would not let it become a topic of discussion. On every occasion, I had raised my hand to support this man in his calling, and I would prove my support by complying totally to his inspired judgment.

Over the next six months, Bishop Hatch and I met each week. He taught me the gospel and challenged me to live its precepts in ways I had never considered. He provided me books to read and even demanded that I read the entire Book of Mormon, which I had never accomplished. Slowly, I came to realize that he was offering me true, caring love, albeit tough love, and that he was genuinely interested in polishing the rough stone of David Beagley into a gem that would become both useful and valuable in the mission field. My experience with Bishop Hatch became a vital exercise in patience and submitting my desires to the will of the Lord. The bishop forced me to measure my standing before God and refuse to settle for mediocre performance or for a causal relationship with Deity. I grew to understand that decisions of great importance, such as serving a mission or marrying for eternity, cannot be approached casually—they require intense preparation. I learned that my timetable was not nearly as crucial as becoming worthy.

When I finally received my mission call to Scotland, I felt prepared. I was well acquainted with the scriptures. I knew how to be obedient to commandments over an extended period of time. I had developed a testimony of sustaining Church authorities even when I didn't agree with their judgments, personalities, or methods. I learned to humbly take counsel, not as a victim, but as one who can exercise agency.

I had no comprehension then how valuable the bishop's tutoring would become to me in the near future. The phrase "waiting upon the Lord" would define my mission experience.

CHAPTER TEN

Scotland, Cysts, and Sorrow

I entered the mission home in Salt Lake City with unbounded enthusiasm. When I crossed into Utah from Arizona, I felt a chill of anxiety.
Although my mother now supported my actions and had even offered
to help fund my mission, I imagined the ridicule that would be heaped
upon me if I encountered my brothers and sisters. Their religion dictated
that zero tolerance be extended to one who had "seen the light" and later
rejected it. Fortunately, my week in the mission home was uneventful
with regard to my family, for in their disavowal of my existence they made
no attempt to visit me. That I would be seven thousand miles away in far
off Scotland was fine with them, and it was just fine with me, too.

When I first set foot in Scotland, the words of the patriarch resounded
in my mind: "You shall be called to be a missionary and serve in foreign
lands." Foreign lands—Scotland! A prophecy fulfilled! My resolve was
strong. I pledged to serve the Lord every minute of every day. I wanted to
be the best missionary in the world, and I knew I could do it. Hard work
was no stranger to me. I knew what it meant to sacrifice everything for
your dreams. I had been schooled in focusing on living difficult commandments over an extended period of time. Within me, I felt prepared and
ready to hit the ground running. I was convinced that the path of faithful
missionary service could only lead me straight to my goal of happiness.

But the road of life is defined by detours.

Shortly after I arrived in Scotland, I developed several cysts on the
lower part of my spine. These large boils soon became sore and would not

heal. They remained open and constantly drained with infected yellow-white fluid. For the first several months, I learned to ignore the pain, but each day the effort became more difficult. I applied fresh medicated pads on the sores twice daily without my companion's knowledge. By the end of each day, my underclothes were always filled with pus and blood. In Scotland, our monthly rent included three meals a day and laundry services. I swore my landlady to secrecy about the blood stains, and I continued to put on a brave face, putting out a 110 percent effort every day. Finally, after eleven months of silent suffering, my pain became so intense that I could neither walk nor ride my bike. Secretly, I made an appointment with a local doctor, who was an acquaintance of my landlady.

"Where's your pain?" the doctor asked.

I gingerly touched the infected area. "Mostly here," I said. I was lying face down on a thin, sheeted table that was covered with what appeared to be butcher paper. Except for a flimsy surgical gown, I was naked. A nurse stood by and appeared underwhelmed when the doctor parted my gown and exposed my backside. Banded to his head was a large, round mirror with a hole in the center for his eye to peer through. When he rotated it into place and flipped a switch, it lighted up. He probed and observed for several minutes while the nurse remained antiseptically stoic.

"Uh-huh," he said, bending down to a new position. I grew uncomfortable.

"What do you see?" I asked.

The doctor straightened, began to remove his gloves, and shook his head. At that point the nurse began to shake her head too as she turned to clean up the examination room.

"You'll need surgery," he said.

"An operation?" My mind raced. I sat up on the table and adjusted my robe. "Isn't there some cream? I don't have time for an operation."

"No. No cream. Surgery is the only option."

"When?" I asked.

"Well, your condition is not life-threatening and basically classified as elective, so there would be no way to schedule the operation for about four and a half months."

"You're kidding! I have to endure this pain for almost five more months?"

"One of the joys of socialized medicine in Scotland," the doctor said. "There is no way to move up the date."

I left the doctor's office, hurting and discouraged. I could barely put one foot in front of the other without shocks of pain shooting down my legs. Every brush of my clothing felt as though hot coals were being placed on my lower back. *I've just got to find a way to quietly gut it out for another year, then get to a hospital when I return to the States,* I thought.

By evening, however, my plan of secretly suffering until I had finished my mission was dashed. How my mission president found out, I never knew, but I suspected that the laundry lady finally became so concerned that she put in a call. She had resorted to separating and washing my clothes from the other laundry because of the increasing amount of blood on my clothing. Recently, she had begun to beg me to see a doctor. The morning after the medical examination, I received a call from my mission president. Pleasantries were exchanged and then came the clincher: "Elder Beagley, I need to see you in my office today. Pack your clothes and come in with your district leader. You are about to be transferred."

My ego said, *You're moving up! You're going to be called as a leader.* But my fear thought, *He's found out! He knows about your problem.* Somehow, deep inside me I knew that the latter was true—my mission president had discovered my secret illness. After packing, my district leader and I rode the double-decker bus to the mission office. I silently played mind games. *If he knows about the cysts,* I thought, *what is the worst that could happen? . . . He could transfer me to the mission home while I recuperate.* That was a sobering thought. I wouldn't be able to tract door-to-door or teach for a while. As I pondered the possibility, I concluded that I could live with that. Other sick elders had spent time in the mission home. Besides, it would be somewhat of a relief to now have my medical problem out in the open. *Not being completely honest with your companion and the mission president constitutes living a lie, doesn't it?* I reasoned. I had kept so many secrets in my youth that the practice seemed quite natural.

The next day, President Jensen, a very kind and gentle man, invited me into his office. He came right to the point. "Elder Beagley," he began, "after much prayer, it has been made clear to me by the Lord that tomorrow morning you are to fly to Salt Lake City, where Church-approved surgeons will perform an operation to help you heal." He left no room for argument, no discussion, no debate. How can anyone argue with, "It has been made clear to me by the Lord"?

I wept. He wept.

"They'll never let me return to Scotland," I said.

"I know."

We cried more.

"I waited as long as I could to tell you," President Jensen said. "I know your passion for missionary work and how you would receive this news. I thought it better to let you know at the very last minute and then send you off."

He was right, of course, but I could neither hide nor deny the pain of having to leave my beloved mission and Scotland. I spent the longest night of my life in a cot in the mission home in Edinburgh. I did not sleep. All I could do was plead with the Lord, "Please don't send me home, not now. I want to stay and finish my mission." Through tears I asked the Lord to consider my difficult teenage years and provide me mercy and healing. I begged for a witness that going home was truly his will. I prayed, waited, and prayed again.

Nothing.

No sweet assurance, no burning of the bosom. I felt alone, forsaken, and abandoned—left to fight through this tragedy by myself.

The next day, as I boarded a jet bound for the eastern coast of the United States and Salt Lake City, I counted the brief months I had served in Scotland—eleven. As the plane lifted off the ground, I stared out the window at the beautiful landscape for which the country is known. It rolled out green before me until it disappeared completely in the mist through which we ascended. Gone. My Scotland was gone. I felt singled out and cheated. Why, of all the missionaries who served in Scotland, was I the one to become ill and be sent away? I could make no sense of it. If God needed to weed out someone, why not a missionary who had taken his call lightly? Or someone who arose late, played around, and counted the days until he could go home to be in the loving arms of family and friends? I was so confused.

Another fear gripped me. What if the Church would not allow me to complete my mission anywhere? What good to them was a missionary in poor health? As I flew the distance of the Atlantic Ocean, I could not conjure one positive thought nor discover one hope. My world had suddenly become very small. If I'd had a flashlight to shine before me on my road of life, it wouldn't have reached past the toes of my shoes. Certainly, the road I had walked had never been lighted beyond a comfortable distance. But I had always clung to the hope that no matter where I was led, happiness was waiting at the end. Now, in midair, with the vast, cold sea below me, I wasn't so sure. Seven thousand miles is a long distance to cry.

CHAPTER ELEVEN

Going Home ... Wherever That Is

In high school, I learned to love working with my hands. Woodwork and welding were activities I especially enjoyed. I became acquainted with different metals and the intensity of heat that was necessary to separate impure matter from stable material. Most metals are measured by their strengths. Raw materials are mined, transported, broken down, melted, and refined. At the zenith of the refinement process, the raw material is heated to the point that nothing impure can remain. At that moment, ingredients are added to ensure that the end product is stronger than the unrefined material could tolerate.

I felt as if the Lord had mined me from the grip of fundamentalism, had transported me to the safe haven of Flagstaff, and had broken me down by a long repentance process. Was my illness and being sent home now a part of the refining process, or was it a punishment? Purifying, testing, strengthening—was I equal to the heat? Could I stand the furnace until God added his special ingredients that would make my soul eternally strong? Just how hot would the refiner's fire become? Within me I believed that God would not suffer me to be tempted or tried above that which I was able; but with the temptation or trial would he also provide a way to escape so that I would be able to bear it? As the jet approached the Salt Lake Airport, I bowed my head and offered a silent prayer that the Lord would strengthen me to endure and to submit to the refining process.

The Scottish mission office had set an appointment for me to see a doctor in Salt Lake City on the Monday following my arrival. They had neglected, however, to notify anyone that I was coming home. Perhaps, because of my unusual family circumstances, they didn't know where home was. My mission papers registered Jerry and Pat as my guardians, but they had moved from Flagstaff to Mesa, Arizona. No other phone number for an immediate family member was available. Consequently, when my plane landed at 10:30 on a Friday night, I found myself standing alone in the Salt Lake Airport with luggage in hand and nowhere to go. I soon located a pay phone and attempted to make a call. All I had were British coins. Frustrated and emotionally frayed, I dialed the operator and asked her to reverse the charges to my mother at her nursing home business in Orem, some fifty miles away.

"David Beagley is calling collect from Salt Lake City," I heard the operator say. "Will you accept the charges?"

I heard my mother say, "Johnny, is that you playing a trick on me again?"

The operator repeated her message and Mom paused. She replied to the operator, "My son David left home years ago and is now serving a mission in Scotland."

Then the operator said to me, "Sir, what would you like me to do?"

By now I was crying so hard that I could barely form the words. "Please, Mom," I gasped, "accept the charges."

Later that night when my dear, sweet mother picked me up at the airport, I wasn't prepared for the rush of emotions that seeing her released in me. I fell into her arms and we both wept. Then, composing herself, straightening, and placing her hands on my shoulders, she looked me over and asked, "Are you okay, David?"

"I must have an operation, Mom," I said. She looked worried. I reasoned, "It's not too serious. I'll be up and about in no time."

Mom didn't appear convinced, but she nodded and said, "All right. Let's get your luggage. We'll talk about it on the way home."

We talked. We talked about my illness. We talked more than we had in years. We spoke of my leaving home at sixteen. For the first time, she told me how badly my departure had hurt her. Seizing the moment, she suggested that my illness might be God's way of reeling me back into the "true religion," that my other brothers and sisters who had stayed faithful to the polygamist group had experienced no such trouble and were all prospering. Surely I could now see the error of my ways. It was evident that in the eleven months that we had been apart, Mom had entrenched herself heavily in the fundamentalist movement. She informed me that she was the Relief Society president in Short Creek and was contributing thousands of dollars each year to better the community there.

For the four years that Mom and I had been apart, our correspondence had been void of doctrinal debates. Despite my weakened body, the spirit within me was strong—strong enough to withstand my mother's barbs. Over recent years and especially during my mission, my testimony had grown from a tiny seed that had been planted at my own mother's knee. It had somehow survived her renouncing all that she taught me; it had survived the oppression of fundamentalism and taken root when I had watched the Spirit change the heart of the Springville policeman. It had budded in the garden of friendship and love in Flagstaff, and blossomed in Scotland. Line upon line, my testimony of the truthfulness of the Church had grown, and now, driving back to Orem, I felt it was time for me to bear that witness to my mother. Once again, my words were guided by the Spirit.

With youthful missionary zeal I said, "Mom, how do you interpret the biblical scripture: 'Go ye therefore, and teach all nations, baptizing them in the name of the Father, and of the Son, and of the Holy Ghost?' "

She shot me a questioning look.

"What is your church doing to fulfill this commandment?" I asked her.

She paused a long time and then replied, "Well, son, my church can't afford to send out an army of missionaries like yours can. We are grateful that your missionaries are baptizing so many people. Your missionaries give converts a portion of the truth and then we can teach them the higher laws of God when they move to Utah."

"What a convenient philosophy!" I said. "You know that the fruits of any true religion have always been based in the sacrifice of missionaries spanning the world to bring people to Christ. Regardless of the threat of persecution, even Jesus sent missionaries into all the world. The history of The Church of Jesus Christ of Latter-day Saints is one of total commitment to missionary service and teaching the restored gospel. How can any church that claims to be true ignore the Savior's commandment to teach every nation? Doesn't Heavenly Father love the people in Scotland or Japan or anywhere around the world as much as he loves your polygamist friends?"

The Spirit was strong. Tears ran down my mother's face. She was left with no defense. She told me how she had once loved the Church and how strong her testimony used to be.

"David," she said, "never lose your conviction."

"What about yours?" I asked.

She gathered herself and her thoughts, then said quietly, "I made my choice a long time ago when I married your dad. My hope for eternal salvation rests with staying true to him. I believe that polygamy is still a valid principle of the gospel."

With that, our debate ended. We had just concluded the first and last doctrinal discussion I would ever have with my mother. My words were firmly rooted in my testimony of continuing revelation from modern-day authorized prophets. Mom's words wavered; she had one foot planted in her former beliefs and the other in polygamy. My dad had put her in that terrible predicament, but she had lacked the faith sufficient to trust that the Lord would take care of her if she left the marriage. My heart went out to her, but I could say nothing to dissuade her. I had fervently hoped that she could have had the courage to leave Dad years ago and return to her pioneer heritage of faith.

The four months that followed were to be defined by surgery, recovery, heartache, and deep reflection. The refiner's fire was melting me down. I longed for Scotland. I wished for peace and happiness. I longed for home, wherever that was. Then, as if the furnace were not hot enough, Patty sent me a "Dear John" letter announcing her engagement to a returned missionary at BYU. I was lying sick in LDS Hospital in Salt Lake City at the time, trying to mend my body, and now my heart was broken. But I was a missionary and could do nothing about her decision. Still, I couldn't stand the searing images of my beloved Patty in someone else's arms. Her life's road had led her to her stated goal: she had found her returned missionary . . . and it wasn't me! Although she lived only fifty miles away in Provo, she would not be coming to the hospital to comfort me in my pain. In fact, the only visitors I had were my mother and a brother, both of whom peppered their conversation with "I-told-you-so's." The other members of my polygamist family still considered me an outcast. For all intents and purposes, I was abandoned, left alone—like Job, I would have to find and rely on my God by myself.

My first surgery was scheduled shortly after I arrived from Scotland. Dr. Dee W. Call was assigned the honor. Dr. Call was a soft-spoken man who performed surgical procedures on missionaries at no charge. He said it was his way of repaying the Lord for all he'd been given.

Dr. Call explained that to rid my body of the cysts that it continued to produce was a rather routine medical procedure. I would be cut open from the bottom of my spine, eight inches downward through my buttocks. Thereafter, the diseased tissue would be removed, and twenty-one stainless steel rings would be used to hold everything together while I healed.

Initially, the operation was deemed a success. For three weeks I lay facedown on a hospital bed with tubes protruding from my body to allow drainage. Then, just as I began to feel hope and regain my strength, two new cysts developed.

"They are open and draining," Dr. Call said sadly after he finished examining me. He shook his head. "Only one in twenty-five of such surgeries are unsuccessful. I've personally never had one fail."

We both shared a long period of discouragement. I asked, "What can be done?"

"Another operation is the only option," he replied. "I'll need to remove more tissue and leave the entire area open for a time to expose the spine. The process of healing will be much slower, but this method of healing, from the inside out, will offer no possibility for diseased tissue to grow."

What could I do? Reluctantly, I submitted to a second surgery. For another three weeks, I either laid on my front or sat on a little rubber tube while soaking in a whirlpool eight times a day. In between the operations, President Jensen wrote to the Church Missionary Committee asking if there was any remote possibility that I might finish my mission in Scotland. The committee finally consented that if the second surgery were successful, they would consider allowing me to return to Scotland. President Jensen forwarded a copy of that letter to me in the hospital, and suddenly my hopelessness faded. I was still wanted; I was still needed. There was light ahead. This trial would have an end. The Lord would heal my wounded body and allow me to return to Scotland to finish my mission—and I would be the best missionary that country had ever known!

During the entire ordeal, Dr. Call had reached out to me and became more than just my surgeon; he became my friend. When I hurt, he felt my pain. He was a caring, loving man. His explanations were not trite or patronizing. He took much time, patience, and compassion to describe each step of the surgeries and what was to be expected during the recovery periods. And so, when he informed me one morning that my second surgery had not proven successful, I was not surprised to find him weeping with me at my bedside. We were friends, not doctor and patient. Our discouragement was beyond what either of us could communicate. He was devastated, and so was I. More cysts were developing and had surfaced. In the medical circle that he walked, a second, more invasive surgery had never proven unsuccessful.

When he left me, I lay alone in my hospital bed, numb. This numbness wasn't a product of any operation from the waist down; it was centered directly in my heart. For the first time in my life, I had no questions for my Heavenly Father. I could think of nothing to say to him. Nothing made sense anymore. The metal of my faith, I thought, had been fired beyond my level of tolerance. I was weary of the refining process. I felt as though everyone and everything on earth and in heaven had let me down and left me alone. I would not be returning to Scotland.

The discouraged mind is fertile soil for the adversary. One expects some mercy when life's circumstances become unbearable. But Satan sees in human pain opportunity—there is no mercy in him. Kicking a person when he is down is his modus operandi. If the devil could hold a gun, he would pull the trigger. Instead, he chips away at every brick in the foundation of a person's faith. The questions and doubts that crossed my mind were depressing and diabolical.

Does God really exist?

If so, are his attributes consistent and perfect?

Does he hear me, see me, know what is going on?

Does he care?

Has he forgotten me?

Had the voice I'd heard in Springville been the figment of my youthful imagination, or was it an actual contact from a heavenly host sent to guide me through a difficult situation?

Is my sickness outside his power to heal?

Is he punishing me?

Did I conjure up my testimony, or can I truly point to irrefutable spiritual evidence that what I believe is the truth?

Over the next few days, Dr. Call reported that my cysts appeared to be lifelong. I attempted to regroup enough to determine if I wanted to abandon God and my faith or remain true to the course that I had chosen. Although I had more questions than answers, I needed to have a reason to move forward. But in which direction? The option of joining my family in the apparent ease and comfort of their polygamist religion had always been held over my head. They had even offered me a good job and a new car if I repented and came back to them. I could return to my fundamentalist brothers and sisters as a hero, proving that "the God of the LDS Church is not dependable as demonstrated by your painful illness and your being sent home from Scotland to endure two unsuccessful operations."

My mind and spirit were discouraged and weary. Taking an easier path that didn't require the mental, emotional, and physical effort became for me a very real consideration. At this very vulnerable time in my life, I remembered the lessons that I had learned in the sugar beet fields: "Never give up . . . hoe to the end of the row." Perhaps, even in that oppressive environment, my brother Larry had performed for me one of the most beneficial character corrections of my life. I was not allowed to give up then, so should I label myself as a quitter now?

I had to respect myself, and no matter how hard it appeared right now, I needed to regroup and plead for a second mission call anywhere the Church chose to send me. I would "hoe to the end of this row" and honor myself and my Father in Heaven.

But it had now become painfully apparent to me that the chances for me serving as a missionary anywhere in the world were slim. Dr. Call had recently received new instructions from the missionary committee: "If Elder Beagley isn't fully healed, send him home." My purpose was clear: I must find a way to convince Dr. Call that I could and should be allowed to serve a mission—somewhere.

In an emotional session in Dr. Call's office, we both were reduced to tears as he explained that my failed surgeries were the only known treatment for the cysts. I pleaded, "If I have to live with them, then let me live with them in Scotland and allow me to complete my mission."

He could not, he said. My cysts were still active, and the instructions from his priesthood leaders were definitive. He had to honor their decision. Was there any room for compromise? I asked. Dr. Call had a little latitude if I was willing to submit.

He would sign my mission papers and state that I was healed sufficiently if I was willing to serve in a nearby mission in the United States. Otherwise, my mission would end on a very sour note. I explained to him that completing an honorable mission was vital to demonstrating to myself and my fundamentalist family that I was not a quitter. I also pointed out that I had no place to call home, so why not allow me to finish my mission?

After I had done a great deal of pleading and made many bold promises, Dr. Call came to a decision. He would allow me a conditional medical release if I would agree to serve the remainder of my mission close to a Church-approved medical facility in the western United States—but not in Scotland! Furthermore, I was to report to him monthly on my progress. I must follow his instructions and do nothing that would further aggravate my condition. The fact that the cysts still existed was a serious concern. Dr. Call made it clear to me that if they didn't heal soon, they could cause lifelong crippling effects.

I agreed to every condition.

When I walked out of Dr. Call's office, my entire body and mind ached. I still felt the physical pain of the surgeries, and I also felt demoralized that both attempts had been unsuccessful. Once again I was alone with no home or supportive family. I felt discouraged that I would not be returning to Scotland. On my register of assets, I could only list that I was still a missionary, but I was depressed at the prospect of serving in a new assignment. Forlorn, humble, raw, I was a shattered human being in a vulnerable and weakened condition. I still felt some anger toward God, but it was softening over time. I was beginning to realize that he was the one and only person who could give me answers and to whom I could turn for love, support, and happiness.

One day, I borrowed my mother's car and drove up Provo Canyon to the same spot that I had camped during the night of my escape. When I arrived, I turned off the headlights and humbly began to plead with Heavenly Father for direction. I needed a respite from Satan's continuing attacks on my faith. I needed strength to attempt another mission in a place that I did not wish to go (although I admitted that any option that allowed me to finish my mission was better than being released). My tears flowed freely. I begged for help to stay firm in my faith. I prayed for over two hours, and when I drove back down the canyon, I left with a meek and humble soul.

I soon received news that the missionary committee had reassigned me to the Northern California Mission. I also learned that the California missions were where all the sick missionaries were sent. As I prepared to depart, I imagined an entire colony of sick missionaries migrating in and out of West Coast hospitals and accomplishing very little missionary work. I wondered if I had the courage to go there. Could I work through the pain and the discouragement? Could I recommit to another mission with the same degree of enthusiasm that I had felt in Scotland? Night and day, I earnestly prayed that I could do so.

As I boarded the train in Salt Lake City, I once more questioned my resolve and my physical capability as I shifted my body on the seat in an attempt to find a way to sit so as to not irritate the cysts. I was not happy; I did not pretend to be. My whole effort now focused on clinging to a thin thread of faith. I tried not to question why God had refused to heal me.

CHAPTER TWELVE

"Patience, My Son. I'm in Charge"

"Why me?" was a question I had asked myself since I was a child growing up in a dysfunctional polygamist family. I continued asking myself that same question during my three years in Arizona, and it now occupied my mind on the train to California.

I knew the question arose from self-pity, but part of it was legitimate. It assumed that my existence did not begin with the conception of my mortal body, but that I had a beginning in another realm with different rules and a different perspective. Somehow, the direction of my life was set long before I received this body—but for what reasons and to what destination I could not perceive. That I was second-guessing God caused me to feel guilty. From the moment I had experienced God's intervention in Springville, I knew that he knew me and was willing to be intimately involved in my life, regardless of my weaknesses. Can anyone answer the question, "Why does God intervene in some situations and not others?" Did I have the right to question him just because I couldn't understand what was happening to me? Had the Savior himself asked the same question, declaring, "Father, why has thou forsaken me?"

I thought, *All things work together for the good of them that love God.*

That scripture rolled around in my mind as I tried to contemplate its implications. I considered that only God could piece together my broken life and create of it something refined, polished, and infinitely valuable.

If the purpose of this mortal life is to gain experience, I pondered, *why do I continue to question the method of that experience when it is offered to me?*

Beyond the Law of Opposition, which we are so quick to quote, do we ignore the Law of Compensation?—that God truly can make everything right and cause all things to work together for our good? I realized that I had created for myself a convenient and dangerous myth. I had imagined that happiness can be attained without conflict or challenges. I considered the Savior, the great exemplar, whom we are to emulate in every way, whose life's path was defined by stones, ruts, and great walls of adversity. Was I "greater than he"? If I truly wanted to be like him and to once again live where he is, was I willing to believe that the path to him was defined by shortcuts?

In the silence of the train car, I bowed my head and prayed with a fervency that I had not experienced since that night in Springville. I did not pray to be delivered from my problems, but rather for strength to bear and to understand them. I wanted to be able to gear up for the challenges that would likely be awaiting me in California. I prayed for a season of respite from the storm, a time to heal spiritually as well as physically and get my feet underneath me again. I wanted to know that I was not alone, that I could face the future with confidence, to know that my Savior had already contemplated my future and had traveled my road before I had arrived, that he had marked my path and would now lead me through the mine fields and beside the still waters. I had always believed that he had overcome the world. Now I prayed for the assurance that he had overcome my world. I begged forgiveness for having constantly questioned his intentions, and I asked for the ability to start over on a new path with a new view and a different environment.

When I concluded my pleadings with the Lord, I found myself alone and in total darkness. The train's passengers and crew had all retired. I looked out the window and saw nothing, not the flicker of city lights, not the coming headlights of highway traffic—nothing. Everything was completely dark and silent. Tears were streaming down my cheeks. My stomach ached from hunger. The not-yet-healed incision down my backside was sore to the touch, and I could not find a comfortable position. I felt so alone in the world and wished someone would come to love and care for me.

Then, like a gentle breeze that kisses spring flowers, I felt a tenderness enter the train and linger where I sat. The presence was almost palpable, and it flowed through my body like a warm fluid. It started at the top of my head and worked its way to the bottom of my feet. It was like a comforting blanket wrapped about my freezing body. I suddenly felt no hunger, no pain, no shame; I had no questions—I only felt peace and gentle compassion.

The seat beside me appeared empty, but literally I felt his loving arms around me, soothing my aching heart. I had never felt the loving arms of my earthly father, but at that moment I knew that my "real" Father now held me close to his bosom and showered his affection freely upon my soul. I was known; I was seen; I was safe.

"Thank you, Father," I said with my head bowed.

And at that very moment, the voice that I had heard in Springville whispered these words, "Patience, my son. I'm in charge."

Sweeter words had never been spoken to me. I focused on the loving declaration of kinship: "My son!" I belonged to someone! I had a relationship with God. I was not here on earth by chance, nor was I simply the biological product of two people who had the ability to physically reproduce. I had been wanted into existence by a divine parent for a godly purpose, and this parent was passionately interested in my mortal welfare and success. I was on a course of life that he knew about and agreed with, and somehow I knew that he had it all worked out. He knew exactly how to move me along to happiness.

For the first time, I realized that never in my life had he let me down. He had always heard my cries. He had always seen my tears. He had always patiently allowed me to stumble and pick myself up. He had sometimes allowed me to struggle through times of crisis, but it had been for a reason. He needed a son whom he knew could be dependable, who had been tested in the fire of conflict and endured the heat. He had stood with me during those difficulties and I could trust him. I had seldom trusted anyone, but I could trust him! I truly had a father!

The touch of my Heavenly Father's caress eventually faded that evening, but the warmth of his love remained. Then and there, I made a decision. I would start anew. I would leave the old David Beagley behind on the railroad tracks. I didn't want him following me to California. I would stuff in his bags the baggage of the childhood scars of polygamy, the discouragement of illness, the grief of leaving Scotland, and the broken heart of losing Patty. I would not allow him to enter my new mission, casting any long shadows, but I would enter with the brightness of hope. God had given me another chance. I could be liberated from every shackle of bondage, and I would stand fast in that liberty wherewith God was making me free. I wanted to start over with a clean slate.

Patience, my son. I'm in charge. I could live on that hope for a very long time!

CHAPTER THIRTEEN

"Go Home and Read Your Patriarchal Blessing"

When the train stopped in Oakland, I was still physically hurting but spiritually and emotionally ready to get started. I was greeted by two elders from the mission home. As one of them threw my luggage into the waiting van, he said that he had picked up several sick missionaries at the train station. His wasn't a cheery comment. Nevertheless, I discarded it and reviewed my resolve to take full advantage of this new opportunity.

My new mission president was a very large man from Rigby, Idaho, named President Peterson. He greeted me with open arms. During our interview I summoned my best missionary enthusiasm (masking my inner reservations) and expressed a burning desire to serve in California. President Peterson was no fool and had obviously held this type of interview before. He simply smiled and sincerely welcomed me to the mission. Then he produced a letter from President Jensen in Scotland complimenting me for my missionary service in that country. I fought back the emotions that were still so near the surface. President Peterson allowed me a moment to compose myself.

"Elder Beagley," he said, "I want you to know that we have been anxiously anticipating your arrival. You are an asset to this mission and the Lord needs your service here. Usually transfers are just a few miles, but the Lord has seen fit to transfer you halfway around the world at great expense. It must be for a good reason. I'm certain, as you give yourself to this important labor, you will bless the lives of many people who might have been touched by no one else—and you will receive some answers that you could not have received in any other situation. You are being assigned to labor in Sacramento as a district leader."

I quickly discovered that missionary work in California and in Scotland were polar opposites. What a change! In Scotland we had to tract all day long. When a discussion was finally taught, we felt as if we had conquered the world. We measured success by the number of discussions taught, not by baptisms. In California, there was no tracting. We taught people all day long, and it wasn't uncommon in our district of six elders to baptize six to ten people a week. As district leader, I spent most of my time interviewing prospective members. I was soon busy and completely caught up in the work. Within days, I felt both relief and confirmation that the answer I had received on the train was truly from the Lord and that my resolve was in accordance with his will. The Lord's work, I came to realize, whether in Scotland or Sacramento, was still the Lord's work. It didn't matter where I labored as long as I put forth my best effort.

I served in Sacramento for four months. My companion was Elder Beasley from Mississippi. Elder Beasley and Elder Beagley! Even we couldn't keep our names straight!

On a Thursday I received a transfer notice in the mail to serve in the Bay Area. I was to become a zone leader. On Friday, as one on my last duties as a district leader in Sacramento, I interviewed a faithful sister for baptism. Her name was Sharon Murphy. She had wanted to be baptized for a very long time. In fact, she had made several serious attempts, but her husband had always refused to sign the consent form. As I gazed into her pleading eyes, I felt impressed to tell her that she would be baptized the next day and to not worry. Her husband would sign the papers.

Both Sister Murphy and I were astonished that I would give her such a promise. She was a woman whose faith and patience had been adequately tested. It was now time for the Lord to say, "It is enough." Later that evening, her husband returned home from a local bar and, in his inebriated state, signed the consent form without hesitation.

On Saturday evening, Sister Murphy came to church dressed in white—beautiful, humble, anxious to be born again. Her father, Robert Boyd, a recent convert, baptized her, and she requested that I confirm her a member of the Church.

While considering the miracle of Sister Murphy's baptism, an incredible thought began to settle on my mind: I was truly a messenger of the Lord and could speak his words with authority. My trials had trained me to submit to his will, and when I acted in his name with deep humility, he would honor what I said. During the darkest days of my adversity, I had felt that I had been making no progress, and all the time the Lord had been spiritually moving me along at a sprinter's pace. I now felt more attuned to the Spirit; I understood better the language of spiritual prompting. I sensed in myself the courage to act on those spiritual impressions. I felt as though blessings were beginning to break loose and flow from what had seemed to be a logjam.

When I placed my hands on Sister Murphy's head to confirm her a member of the Church, I scanned the audience and my eyes fell upon a young woman whom I had never seen before. Again, the Spirit's voice sounded in my mind, "Find out about her after the meeting."

At the conclusion of the confirmation, after shaking hands and exchanging congratulations, I approached the young lady and asked her name. "Roberta Boyd," she said. "I'm the sister of the woman who was baptized today."

"Are you a member of the Church?" I asked.

"No, thank you. And I never will be. I'm only here because my dad asked me to come." If her tone was meant to startle or to put me at a distance, it didn't work.

The Spirit whispered again, "Find out about her."

"I've met many of your family," I said. "How many children do your parents have?"

"Six."

"And how many are members of the Church?"

"Five," she muttered.

I decided to be bold. "So what's your problem?"

That broke the ice. She couldn't make her face remain stern-looking and cold. First she sputtered, then she laughed.

We both began to laugh. I handed her my missionary card with my name on it.

"You need to keep this," I said.

"I'll think about it," she replied, teasingly.

When my companion and I excused ourselves, I turned to her, and in a parting shot said, "After you have thought about it—and humbled yourself—give me a call."

She tried to conceal a smile, but I could tell I had made a connection.

The next day was Sunday and the last Sabbath that I was to spend in Sacramento. It was the mission policy to fellowship new converts, so Elder Beasley and I attended Sister Murphy's ward. To my amazement and joy, I discovered that Roberta Boyd had accepted an invitation from her father to honor him on Father's Day. She had come so that the entire family would be together. After the meeting, Roberta walked up to me.

"You've got a pretty direct approach when you talk to people," she said.

"You too," I replied.

She laughed.

"Where'd you learn it?" she asked.

I tried to think of a clever answer. "Good upbringing, I guess. All that hard farm work."

She eyed me and said, "Okay, farm boy. I'm ready."

"Ready for what?"

"I want to receive the missionary discussions."

Our kidding each other suddenly stopped and our conversation became serious.

"You're sure?" I asked.

She nodded her head. "Yes."

The humility in her voice told me that she had recently felt something and hungered to know more.

"My companion and I would be honored to teach you," I said.

My transfer was set for Tuesday morning. Monday, my regular preparation day, was supposed to be for doing laundry and packing for my transfer. However, I could not pass up a golden contact, someone so eager to learn about the gospel of Jesus Christ, especially someone who had turned down the missionaries so many times before.

Elder Beasley and I set up a time on Monday evening to teach Sister Boyd the first discussion. We arrived at 7:30. Roberta's teasing personality surfaced again as we entered her apartment. "Would you like a cup of tea?" she bantered, knowing very well the Church's stance on such things. We brushed it off with a good laugh.

"Are you ready to learn?" I asked.

She became serious and said, "Yes."

The missionary discussions began with a review of the personality of the Godhead and the calling of Joseph Smith as a prophet. My companion and I taught Roberta about the reality of a loving Heavenly Father who was separate and distinct from his Only Begotten Son, Jesus Christ. We also related the beautiful story of young Joseph's quest for the true church, which led him to the Sacred Grove. When we came to the part where we were to ask her to express her feelings about the restored gospel, she wept and said, "I know that what you are telling me is true."

Roberta told us that from the time her parents had joined the Church, she had masked the spiritual promptings that she had received concerning the Church. But she could deny them no longer. Now she wanted to be the final member of her family to be baptized and unite them all in the gospel of Jesus Christ. Hers was one of the most spectacular changes of heart that I had ever witnessed. It was as though I could actually see the Holy Ghost descend upon her and open her mind.

At the end of our discussion, we explained that in order to be baptized she would need to complete the six missionary discussions and ask her Father in Heaven if her decision to join the Church was right. She smiled bashfully, like a little girl, and said, "But I don't know how to pray. Will you teach me?"

"Of course we will teach you," I replied humbly.

Elder Beasley and I taught her the four steps of prayer.

Roberta offered a simple but beautiful prayer. It was her first vocal prayer to her Heavenly Father. Her words conveyed one of the most humble approaches to God I had ever heard. Then, to my astonishment, during the prayer I felt the Spirit whisper to me, "Go home and read your patriarchal blessing."

CHAPTER FOURTEEN

The Puzzle Pieces Begin to Fit

My patriarchal blessing was one of my most prized possessions. Over the years, I had referred to it often for comfort and direction. Especially during hard times I had felt great strength from its promises. Now, the Spirit had prompted me to read my blessing again with humility and prayer. After having completed the missionary discussion with Roberta Boyd and hearing her beautiful prayer, Elder Beasley and I returned to our apartment, where I was to finish packing for my transfer. I felt the need to be alone, and I asked my companion for that opportunity. Shutting the bedroom door, I sifted through my papers until I found my patriarchal blessing. A sense of anticipation stirred within me. The only real father that I had even known, the creator of my spirit, had a message for me in my blessing.

As I began to read, I felt as though a panoramic view of my life was presented to my mind—the oppression of my childhood, the search for identity and belonging, first love, the pain of illness, discouragement, confusion, and ultimately submission. I imagined that I was standing on a long road that had been defined by harsh ruts and detours, but now it had the faint image of a distant goal in view. What had I sought these long years? I knew the answer. I wanted the happiness that comes from a nurturing relationship between a father and a son. This earth life had not provided me with a father whom I could love and cherish, but I had fostered a happy, trusting relationship with my Heavenly Father, a relationship that I could turn to daily. I no longer desired to be free from problems along the road of life, but just to find happiness and joy in the journey. A gradual warm assurance welled within me as though my loving Heavenly Father were saying, "I've heard your every prayer. I've seen your every tear. It's enough. You've paid the price necessary to receive the reward."

I carefully pored over each word of my blessing with new resolve. I tried to feel impressions as I read and reread every phrase. I especially focused on references to missionary work, for it was a subject that occupied my mind since I had first been called to Scotland. I thrilled at the promise: "The time will come when you shall be called in the foreign lands to preach the gospel, and you shall be fluent in speech, and the Holy Ghost shall direct you to the doors of those who have been praying for the light. The Holy Ghost will carry your testimony into the hearts of those you teach, and you shall be magnified in their sight, and truly they shall testify that you are a man of God."

Surely it had been so.

As I read more, my heart began to pound within my chest. The following words seemed to leap off the page and fill me with awe and confirmation: "Through your great services as a missionary, you shall be directed to a sweet and virtuous woman. She shall sustain you in your noble ideals, and she shall be an inspiration to you. The Spirit shall whisper to you that she is to be your wife, and you shall take her to the house of the Lord and be married for time and all eternity. Sweet and obedient children shall be sent into your home, and they shall carry your name with distinction and with honor; and shame shall not be associated with your name. There shall come into your home prophets of the Lord, and they shall dine at your table, and you shall feast upon your blessings that they shall leave upon you and your family."

The paragraph was not new to me. In fact, Patty and I, during moments of amorous anticipation that we would someday be married, had read these same words and attempted to plan our future around them. Our interpretation called for Patty's supporting me through her letters during my mission. Then, we supposed, we would be "directed" to each other and marry in the house of the Lord. But now, since Patty was directed somewhere else, I had considered this part of my blessing uninspired and had effectively discarded it, as if one could amputate a limb and still call the body whole. Ignoring the words had become easier for me than dealing with the confusion and hurt of losing Patty. I had fantasized receiving a letter any day now in which Patty would plead to return and express her regret for ever straying. That God was capable of restoring what I thought was lost or that he could still keep his promises were concepts I was still trying to rebuild in my mind.

Reading the words of my blessing now, I could not deny the Spirit, and the evidence seemed to be mounting that my Father was fully cognizant of what his patriarch had said. For years, he had been leading me carefully down a path to fulfill those promises every whit. I felt overwhelmed and stunned by my Heavenly Father's immediate goodness and constant awareness of me, that he was a God of truth and could not lie, that he honors the words spoken through proper authority, and that he has the power to move mountains or divert rivers out of their paths in order to accomplish his purposes. I felt so small and humble.

But I had no room in my life for a woman. When Patty had chosen to turn her attention to another, I had resolved to wait several years after the completion of my mission before I entangled myself in another amorous web. Quietly, I said to myself, "Missionaries aren't supposed to meet their future spouses on their missions."

But I read and re-read the words again: "Through your great services as a missionary, you shall be directed to a sweet and virtuous woman. She shall sustain you in your noble ideals, and shall be an inspiration to you. The Spirit shall whisper to you that she is to be your wife, and you shall take her to the house of the Lord and be married for time and all eternity."

My mind filled with a flood of questions.

Was I willing to interpret these words any other way?

Was I willing to discount the promptings I was receiving from the Spirit?

Could I just change gears and involve myself with a stranger whom I knew nothing about?

I was a missionary! This was the wrong time and place! How could I concentrate on missionary work with this piece of information?

I barely knew Roberta Boyd. I certainly had no feelings for her. As a missionary, I had trained myself not to allow my mind to wander. Young Scottish lassies were overbearing in their efforts to brand a wealthy American missionary as their own. My defenses were well tutored and positioned for bachelorhood.

I was scheduled to be transferred the next day. What could I possibly do?

This whole thing was so confusing. I suddenly felt like mourning more than rejoicing. I felt like Adam who had been given two conflicting commandments—in order to live one he had to transgress the other. My mission had been filled with so many conflicting and unusual twists and turns, and just as normalcy was returning to me . . . boom! Here was another unexpected road block. My first inclination was to set my patriarchal blessing aside and ignore it completely. By so doing, I imagined, the confusion and uncertainty might just go away. During my childhood I had learned the art of ignoring many things. Now, however, a constant and more persistent voice was screaming in my head, "You had better work through this one, because it could be a life-altering event."

Certainly I had enjoyed teaching Sister Boyd. Her depth of sincerity and conversation had touched me and had become one of the focal moments of my mission. She was short, about five feet tall, brunette, cute, and had a bubbly personality. Throughout my teenage years, as a young man will, I had envisioned marrying a tall, five-foot-ten-inch blonde with striking measurements. Sister Boyd didn't exactly fit that model. Besides, I wasn't in the market! My mind was riveted on doing the Lord's work. I had paid too dear a price for this mission and I was not about to be distracted. Every day that I was able to work I considered it a blessing.

I was driving myself crazy with my ruminating. I stood and paced my bedroom floor. I realized that, using Joseph Smith as a model, only an appeal to God could answer the questions. My Father in Heaven was the source of the information; he would also have to be the source of the answer and the direction I should take. I went to my knees and bowed my head. With humility and trust, I poured out my soul for understanding. I prayed, "Heavenly Father, what do the words of my blessing mean? Am I hearing the voice of thy Spirit or am I being deceived by misguided impressions? Is Roberta Boyd someone whom thou wants me to know? And how is that possible given the calling that I have?"

I waited, pondering, listening, not wanting to force God's hand. I knelt quietly at the foot of my bed with my eyes closed for almost thirty minutes. I felt assured that my Father had heard my prayer, but I felt no answer. I stood and paced again, reconsidering my prayer and how I was asking. I said to myself, "Nothing else in this life has come easily, so I must ask once more but with more resolve and more urgency."

I knelt by the bedside and again poured out my heart to the Lord. Expressing great trust in his ability to answer my questions, I pled for guidance in correctly interpreting my patriarchal blessing. The more I cried unto the Lord, the more I struggled in both body and soul. I ached with desire for communication. Clenching my hands together, I fought to bring myself into line so that every molecule of my body was focused upon being single to that purpose. Exhausted, I stopped pleading and waited. Inside my beat-up heart I hoped I would receive the answer to just set Roberta Boyd aside and finish my mission. That path would have been much simpler understandable.

As a boy, I loved to put together puzzles. They were the simple kinds, and I could fit the pieces in place with relative ease. Later, when I attempted more complex puzzles, my concentrated effort often required several days before I could even figure out one piece. Sometimes I worked on puzzles for weeks before the big picture would emerge.

I was not the architect of my life's puzzle. Over the years, I felt that I had only been an observer, that other powers were moving and fitting together the pieces. I recognized no semblance of a beautiful picture. All had seemed a jumble of colors and undefined shapes. I could not make out the boundaries or determine why some pieces were seemingly being shoved into place, moved around, or not fitting at all. I had more questions than answers and could not seem to force clarification no matter how hard I tried. All I had ever wanted was for the puzzle to come together into a clear portrait of happiness, but the pieces had appeared so disjointed and the goal so remote. I had experienced seasons of joy in California and elsewhere, but nothing consistent. I felt is if I had lived my life with one eye gazing down the road of hope and the other eye glancing over my shoulder for what obstacle might blindside me next.

I was absolutely taken aback by the words that I was reading in my patriarchal blessing. I knew that the prompting I had felt to return home and read it was from my Father. I also knew he was attempting to position some missing puzzle pieces of my life so that I could clearly understand them. But why now? What should I do with this knowledge? Who could I tell? And what about Roberta Boyd? We had only been acquainted for three days . . . and I was leaving Sacramento tomorrow!

Since experiencing Heavenly Father's loving caress on the train to California, I had learned to listen quietly for his instruction. Often these directions came in the form of gentle whispers. No trumpet or audible voice, but whispers. Sister Murphy's experience had produced such a moment. One line from my blessing now loomed large: "The Spirit shall whisper to you . . ." The pleadings of my prayers were finished, so I sat quietly at the edge of my bed to listen. I had no doubt that my prayers would be answered. While waiting, I opened my scriptures and read the words: "Then shall thy confidence wax strong in the presence of God; and the doctrine of the priesthood shall distill upon thy soul as the dews from heaven." Then directly and quietly I heard a voice whisper the familiar words, "Patience, my son. I'm in charge. I brought you this far for this very reason."

Mother had often read to us children the stories from the Bible. The love story of Jacob and Rachel seemed so different from the demonstrations of love that I observed in my world. In Short Creek, I had seen so many marriages that had been arranged, with little consideration for the couple's dating or enjoying an engagement period. When I had separated myself from that lifestyle, I vowed that when I chose my mate I would give myself months for careful planning and full latitude for personal choice.

Now, reading my blessing, I wondered if a greater power had interrupted agency and had assigned me my future mate. My upbringing colored my feelings.

Did my blessing state what could be or what had to be?

Did my Heavenly Father really have the ability to look into the future and see my life?

Was it possible that, because of my skeptical nature, I needed the assistance of a heavenly parent to make this most important decision of my life?

Did I have to consider this decision at such an untimely moment?

Had I really had to give up everything, including my mission in Scotland, which I loved so much, for this very reason?

The words, "I have brought you this far for this very reason" pounded in my ears. I knew for a certainty that they were not my words, nor were they the words of the adversary—my prayerful pleadings had been pure and sincere.

But what about Sister Boyd? Had the Lord bothered to pass any of this knowledge on to her? Was the Spirit working on her as it was me? What if she looked into my background and determined that my family's history was more than she could handle? That would be a problem for any worthy young lady.

What in the world was I to do with this piece of information? There was no way I could go to my companion and say, "Hey, I just met my future wife tonight." Besides being Elder Beasley's companion, I was his district leader. What kind of example would I be setting? As I considered my dilemma, I reasoned that since I was being transferred to become a zone leader, I needed to act like a leader. I needed someone whom I could trust to hear my story. I needed President Jensen, but he was in Scotland. Could I trust my new mission president as much? Could I tell him the things that I locked up deep in my heart and ask him to cherish them? Once more, the issue of trust haunted me. If I truly believed that he was the duly appointed servant of God in California, then I must trust him! Once again I would venture out and place my heart in the hands of another and pray that it wouldn't be trampled.

The next day, when I arrived in the mission home, I would lay the entire issue before President Peterson. Holding the keys of presidency, he was the one person who could give me the Lord's counsel. The thought entered my mind that the timing of this transfer, which gave me an opportunity to meet with my priesthood leader, could not be accidental. I could discount it as coincidence, but the Spirit whispered that all had been planned by a higher source.

When I finally emerged from my bedroom that night, I found my companion asleep on the couch. It was after 1:00 a.m. As I stood there, I thought about the phrase in my blessing that said, "And shame shall not be associated with your name." I had grown up in the shadow of shame and ridicule. Now those words penetrated my heart. Perhaps the future was bright. I bowed my head in silent prayer and asked that President Peterson would be inspired in giving the advice I would seek from him the following day.

The next morning I boarded a bus for Oakland. I would stay in the mission home that evening and then transfer to San Mateo the next day. After the evening meal with President and Sister Peterson and the mission home staff, I made my way to the president's office with my patriarchal blessing tucked in my suit pocket. I found him alone. He smiled when he looked up from his paperwork.

"What can I do for you, Elder Beagley?" he asked.

"May I have a few minutes of your time?" I replied. "I have a troubling matter that is concerning me."

He motioned me into his office and I closed the door. He greeted me with open arms. During my bus ride and the time I had spent in the mission home, I had determined not to preempt any discussion by first expressing my feelings. I reasoned that by doing so I would prejudice the advice he might give me. Instead, I just handed him my patriarchal blessing.

"Will you read it?" I asked.

"Yes. Of course."

I waited nervously as he accepted the pages and settled back in his chair. He didn't read the blessing quickly, but seemed to ponder each sentence and phrase. His face appeared solemn. At times, I thought I detected a slight nod or the furrowing of his brow. He read and then re-read the part about my mission. He rubbed his chin and raised an eyebrow, but he never looked up until he had finished. Finally, he set the pages gently on his desk and smoothed them. Then he looked at me over his big desk and stared directly into my eyes. He was a big, imposing man weighing well over three hundred pounds. I felt small and suddenly afraid. I was sure that I was about to receive the lecture of my life on the topic of remaining focused on my mission and leaving the issue of the opposite sex alone until I returned home and could do something about it.

Time seemed to stand still. I began to fidget and my hands felt cold. At length he looked me directly in the eye and asked, "Have you met her, Elder?"

"Yes, President," I said, forcing out the words. "I believe I have."

"And you're confused," he said, as if he were anticipating what I would say next.

"Yes."

"Have you told her or anyone else about what it says in your blessing?"

"No."

Having learned as a child to speak only when spoken to was a lesson that I now utilized to guide me through a very difficult conversation. He grew quiet and looked away. I waited.

"I will need some divine help in order to give you proper advice," he said.

When he knelt beside his desk, I also went to my knees. Then, from his lips, I heard offered one of the most sincere pleadings for heavenly intervention that I had ever imagined possible. President Peterson prayed so humbly for help that any doubt I harbored of his prayer being heard fled my mind. When he finished, he asked me to pray. With the best language I could rally, I cried out for direction and for instruction to come through my priesthood leader. We prayed together for almost thirty minutes. Then, when we stood, he took me in his big arms and said, "What has happened to you, Elder Beagley, is of God. You should go back to Sacramento and be the one to interview Sister Boyd to become a member of the Church."

"Go back to Sacramento?" I asked.

"Just for her interview and baptism. One of my assistants will accompany you."

Then he became very serious. "For now," he continued, "this revelation should be kept between you, me, and the Lord."

I agreed. President Peterson relaxed, smiled, and sat down in his chair. For the next few minutes we both expressed our marvel at how the Lord deals with his children. As I stood to leave, he put an arm around me and said, "You have a sacred calling as a missionary and a zone leader. The Lord has revealed this information to you at this time as evidence of his great trust in you. It is imperative that you accomplish and finish your mission with honor."

As we parted, he gave me permission to write Sister Boyd once every week, even though she lived within the boundaries of our mission. I was to keep our letter writing to myself.

The following weekend, I returned to Sacramento and interviewed Roberta "Bobbi" Boyd for membership in The Church of Jesus Christ of Latter-day Saints. I felt such joy! During the interview, we both expressed our love for the Lord and our determination to obey his commandments. With tears of gratitude, she responded affirmatively and with conviction to each of the baptismal questions. Her heart was pure and beautiful. I said nothing to her about my patriarchal blessing. That would have to wait. The only thing that mattered now was Bobbi's membership in the Church. Her conversion and the promises that still lay before us caused me more joy than I had ever known. All my feelings of fear and shame had fled with President Peterson's assurance that it was of God.

Bobbi's father baptized her, and I gave her a blessing confirming her a member of the Church. Later that evening, after the baptism, I returned to San Mateo, where I threw myself into the work of the Lord. Every week, Bobbi and I exchanged letters. The more I grew to know her, the more I marveled at Heavenly Father's miraculous power to shape me and to lead me carefully down a rocky path. I began to see the pieces of the puzzle of my life come together. Never could I have chosen such a jewel for my eternal companion. As I received each of her letters, the Spirit assured me that Heavenly Father had considered and accepted the sacrifices of my youth and had paved the way years earlier to bring me to the point of making the most important decision of my life. I could not express enough gratitude to God. What I had prayed for unceasingly—that which had always seemed so far away—now appeared within my grasp. I was happy—happy to be a productive missionary, happy that I had a Father who knew and loved me, happy that my future held such incredible promise.

Bobbi's letters revealed that she was determined to be obedient to the Lord. She thirsted for spiritual knowledge and loved the Church. Each week when I sat down to write her, I wanted so badly to share the promises about "us" in my patriarchal blessing, but I knew that by doing so I would be taking away her moral agency. I would have to wait until I had been released as a missionary. Until then, we could only develop our friendship. In the back of my mind I entertained the fear that perhaps she wouldn't have the same feelings for me, or that somehow I wouldn't measure up to her standards. I also knew that such fears demonstrated a lack of faith in God's eternal plan.

For now, Bobbi's friendship was enough.

CHAPTER FIFTEEN

Finishing Strong

The final months of my mission were some of the most productive. I was filled with absolute and continuous awe at the Lord's love for his children. Although my cysts remained and were often open and painful, I had learned to work around the inconvenience, never allowing them to dictate how I would serve. As I had previously promised Dr. Call, I followed his prescribed medical treatment and remained in touch with him. Thus, the last part of my mission flew by, and all too soon it was coming to a close. From the time Bobbi and I had begun to correspond, her letters had been full of encouragement and support, which I recognized as yet another fulfillment of my patriarchal blessing: "She shall support you in your noble ideals, and she shall be an inspiration to you."

I was yet an observer of the Lord's miracles. As a missionary, I could do nothing else. I watched Heavenly Father orchestrate the events of my life and cause the promises of my patriarchal blessing to be realized. I gained a deep appreciation for Bobbi's intelligence, devotion, and obedience. She took it upon herself to understand the mission rules and was not willing to compromise me in the slightest degree. When she discovered the rules of letter writing within the mission, she contacted President Peterson to be certain that she and I had his permission to write once a week. She received his assurance.

As if the Lord wanted to tie a ribbon around the beautiful gifts that he was showering upon me, I received the welcome news that my mother wished to come to Oakland and pick me up at the completion of my mission. I had missed her. Having crossed the world bearing witness of the Lord and his restored gospel, I deemed it a great opportunity to once again bear testimony to my mother of the truthfulness of the Church. I would have a captive audience! She would have to listen to me all the way to Utah. I wanted to share with her my patriarchal blessing and its promises, to demonstrate the Lord's hand in my life. I hoped this would cut through all the prejudices and pain of her polygamist lifestyle and that she would desire to return to the true and living Church.

When she saw me, we embraced. Only the reunion that occurs as souls pass into the next world could exceed what my mother and I experienced as we held each other and wept. Soon, she stepped back and scanned me as a mother will, and asked, "Are you okay?" She referred to my continuing health concerns.

"Much better," I replied. She eyed me suspiciously, and I added, "I'll tell you everything. We have lots of time."

Disneyland was our destination—Southern California—just me and Mom. And then another miracle happened. One week before the completion of my mission, President Jensen, my Scottish Mission President, called to inform me that he was being reassigned to the Los Angeles Mission. The Brethren had combined the two Scottish Missions into one, and David B. Haight would be the new mission president. President Jensen wanted to know if I would come to visit him. Again, I was amazed at the Lord's timing and his goodness. When Mother and I arrived at the mission headquarters in Los Angeles, I felt as though God had sent my second dad to California so that we could be together again.

President Jensen handed me an envelope containing $500 of his personal money. We wept. I knew that I could trust him with the precious truths of my patriarchal blessing. Without shame, but with extreme pride, knowing that my earthly life was being monitored and guided, I handed President Jensen my blessing. After reading it carefully, he spoke words that were identical to President Peterson's. "Have you met her, Elder Beagley?" he asked.

I related to him my experience in meeting Bobbi. Now he and I both had a clearer understanding about why, despite our best efforts, I had needed to leave Scotland. We wept together a second time. We were no longer president and elder, but father and son, and he had always treated me so.

I returned to Orem, Utah, and said good-bye to Mother. Our ride together had produced pleasant conversations. I had been able to express my firm conviction of the gospel of Jesus Christ. I testified to her with the boldness of a young missionary. Then I traveled home to Flagstaff, Arizona, to spend one week visiting friends and loved ones. Next, I traveled to Mesa, where Jerry and Pat had moved.

Through great difficulty, I had completed an honorable mission for the Lord. Now it was up to me to return to California and begin building the foundation for a home and life that would last for eternity. I felt that I had a third mission back in California, and it was the most important of my life. Released and free to pursue personal goals, I could now court the wonderful woman whom my Heavenly Father had chosen as my eternal companion.

While serving in San Mateo, California, I had befriended a very missionary-minded bishop by the name of Stan Roberts. He invited me to spend eight months living in his home and working at his manufacturing and painting plant. Bobbi and I had decided to date for those months to get to know one another better. If marriage was in our future, we both only wanted it to happen in a temple. Being a recent member of the Church, Bobbi would not be eligible for a temple recommend for one full year from her baptismal date. It seemed a small sacrifice for an eternity together. For the next several months, I worked for Bishop Roberts during the week and, on the weekends, I borrowed his car to travel one hundred miles to be with Bobbi Boyd in Sacramento.

My love for this beautiful woman grew with every moment we spent together. She brought meaning to my life and prospects of joy to my future. Her discovery of gospel principles allowed us no room for compromise in their observance. I had to be at my very best to match her spiritual efforts. One evening, following her acceptance of my marriage proposal, when the Spirit whispered to me that the time was right, I handed Bobbi my patriarchal blessing and asked her to read it. Once again, I chose not to prejudice her with my interpretation of its contents. No words can express the joy that we both felt knowing that the God of heaven had looked down upon the two of us, his mortal children, and sealed our union. Both of us were grateful that we had passed the necessary tests in life that would allow us the fulfillment of such promises.

Bobbi and I were sealed in the Salt Lake Temple on May 27, 1966. My mother's father and my brother, Jerry, and his wife, Pat, were the only members of my family present that day. Bobbi's parents and two of her aunts represented her family. Stan and Fran Roberts flew from San Mateo, California, to stand in the place of my parents.

.

Epilogue

My story has no ending. In all the ways that are eternally important, my story was just beginning. During the portion of my life covered in this book, I was given the unique opportunity of perspective. There was a scripture in the Book of Mormon, in Ether 12:6, that was never far from my mind: "And now, I Moroni, would speak somewhat concerning these things; I would show unto the world that faith is things which are hoped for and not seen; wherefore, dispute not because ye see not, for ye receive no witness until after the trial of your faith."

When I looked back down the road I had traveled in my youth, I saw turns and detours that appeared to have no purpose or meaning. I also saw the unmistakable hand of Providence leading me on and encouraging me. When my father embraced polygamy, my road took a turn that shattered my childhood. But my first father, the creator of my spirit, stood beside me and sent good friends to preserve the option of the gospel in my life. Later, he helped me escape an oppressive home life.

In Springville, Utah, my road detoured again when all hope for escape seemed to vanish in the image of the policeman. Heavenly Father stepped in again, spoke to my mind the exact words to say to him, and softened the officer's heart. From that experience I learned that even though I had been deprived of an earthly father, my Heavenly Father who knew and loved me was near.

My path hit a bump at the stake patriarch's home when I began to discount his words and his priesthood calling. I saw him as only a man.

But God seemed to say, "Listen to what he's telling you; it comes straight from me!" I would later discover that every word was inspired.

In Flagstaff, my journey needed a course correction. My inspired bishop exercised some tough but genuine love to help me take the commandments seriously and prepare me for an honorable mission. When I felt like rebelling, the Spirit whispered, "Be submissive; be wise; hold on your way."

My road seemed to hit a dead end the night I urgently prayed in the mission home in Scotland for healing and to remain. But it was to no avail. It was as though God was saying, "I'm sorry that you feel sad about leaving your mission in Scotland, but you'll gain needed strength by being alone tonight. You will better appreciate what I have in store for you in California if you endure the struggle."

At the hospital in Salt Lake, I could see no purpose to my life's journey at all. My whole attention was riveted upon the moment. I was left alone to work out what I believed and how deeply I believed it.

My road to Oakland, California, was defined by the train rails that spanned the Nevada desert. Why my road had taken such a hard turn, I did not know. But after much mental anguish and crying out to God, I heard the words, "I know what you're feeling, so I will send an extra portion of my love to comfort you. Patience, my son, I'm in charge."

And finally, all the bending roads and confusing pathways of my life's journey converged in Sacramento as I read my patriarchal blessing and felt God saying, "Now you're beginning to see the big picture. Your sacrifice has been accepted and your obedience will be rewarded. Hold on a little longer and I'll allow you to marry her."

The result of my life's journey had become perfectly clear: true happiness comes from the arms of a loving Heavenly Father. Happiness was also his goal for me. I discovered that eternal joy is only achieved through waiting on the Lord, because he alone knows the eventual outcome of our lives.

In the years that have followed since our wedding, Bobbi and I have become best friends. She is my love and the light of my life. Together, we have been blessed with six beautiful children and nineteen wonderful grandchildren, who have remained faithful to the Lord. Bobbi still radiates the same enthusiasm, grace, and beauty that I saw in her thirty-six years ago when I first met her.

Bobbi and I live in the heart of Utah and love all of my brothers and sisters, whether or not they are members of the Church. Today, my family members—those who still practice polygamy and those who are members of The Church of Jesus Christ of Latter-day Saints—are torn apart by religious bigotry. The polygamist community has shattered into many different factions. Some of my brothers and sisters are caught up in this and hate others of their siblings. Often they are forbidden or refuse to acknowledge kinship to one another. The love of Christ, which they all claim to espouse, has lost its luster as they scream religious differences at each other. My efforts to achieve any family unity have been met with harsh resistance by both sides. It seems that no matter how many sermons are preached in LDS chapels or in polygamist halls, hatred rears its ugly head.

Lacking the ability to trust others was a deficit of character that I learned in my youth. Trust was what God determined to teach me. He continuously placed me in situations where I could not wiggle free. Time after time, when deliverance came, I had to make a decision about who or what had rescued me. Discounting the "little" miracles as luck was too easy. But, when more urgent things happened, it became harder for me to ignore the emancipating hand of God. Trust, I came to understand, is the highest manifestation of love. For many years following my departure from polygamy, God spoon-fed me evidences that he was perfectly trustworthy and absolutely dependable. He patiently reprogrammed my skeptical, sarcastic, untrusting mind to become one that was more apt to be believing rather than doubtful and fearful. I came to understand that by placing obstacles along my path, which only he could help me overcome, he could help me face and defeat the monster of mistrust. He never disappointed me—not once. He never destroyed my delicate faith.

What about the cysts?

Waiting on the Lord took on greater meaning after Bobbi and I began courting. During my mission in California, I discovered that if I rode in a car, rather than on a bike as I had done in Scotland, I could control much of the pain. The dozen cysts that had plagued me and had necessitated two operations became two cysts when Bobbi and I started dating. Their discharges had diminished greatly by that time. Three weeks after I returned to California I was called up by the U.S. Selective Service for a physical examination. They took one look at my open cysts and promptly declared me 4-F. I would not be going to Vietnam. Perhaps that was a trial that Heavenly Father wanted to spare me. Four weeks after the examination, both cysts stopped draining and the wounds closed. They remain so today and have never returned. Evidently, the Lord had used the cysts to serve a purpose, and once I had learned what I needed to know, he chose to end that test in my life. Once more, I was in awe at the wisdom, awareness, and love of a caring, trustworthy Heavenly Father.

Too often, we focus only on what we can immediately see in the predictable future. When life's events turn unpredictable, we tend to blame God and become skeptical. *Why would a loving God put me through this?* we ask ourselves. Our future salvation depends upon how each of us answers that question.

Our Heavenly Father knows what the future holds. I know that for a fact. He wants nothing more than to see us fight through each of life's struggles and to achieve eternal happiness in his presence. But this reward must be earned through the heat of the refiner's fire. Sometimes God's mortal children choose to find "cooler places" to avoid the intensity of the flame. How it must hurt him to see us choose an easier path. His eternal joy comes through the exaltation of each and every one of his children. There can be no happiness when, through our own actions, we settle for less than what we are capable.

I am certain that we will all have the opportunity to look back upon this life as if we were watching one big video, and then we will be able to assess how well we made decisions at critical junctions.

In my case, I sincerely believe that because I was deprived of a mortal father to guide me through critical junctions, my Heavenly Father set up a pathway to success. If I could endure, submit to him, and trust his judgment as my Father, he would reward me with one of his most precious daughters, whom I could love and cherish throughout this life and eternity. So often I wanted to give up and go the easier way. But I could not. At such times, the Holy Ghost played a critical role in my life. He was sent to me to counter the barbs of Satan and bolster my faith. I am so thankful that I had the courage to listen to that sweet Spirit, to submit to the will of my eternal Father, and wait on the Lord.

Please know that he is near and that he is in charge.

About the Author

David LaMar Beagley was born in 1944 in Provo, Utah, to Jesse and Althea Beagley. He was the tenth of twelve children. At age sixteen, he ran away from his polygamist home in Utah and joined the LDS Church in Flagstaff, Arizona.

He married Roberta Boyd in the Salt Lake Temple on May 27, 1966. They are the parents of six children and have nineteen grandchildren. He graduated from Southern Utah State University in 1970 and moved to Idaho Falls, Idaho, to begin his twenty-year career in the Seminary Department of The Church of Jesus Christ of Latter-day Saints.

0 26575 52040 8